Psychology Express

Occupational Psychology

The PsychologyE✕press series

→ UNDERSTAND QUICKLY
→ REVISE EFFECTIVELY
→ TAKE EXAMS WITH CONFIDENCE

'All of the revision material I need in one place – a must for psychology undergrads.'
Andrea Franklin, Psychology student at Anglia Ruskin University

'Very useful, straight to the point and provides guidance to the student, while helping them to develop independent learning.'
Lindsay Pitcher, Psychology student at Anglia Ruskin University

'Engaging, interesting, comprehensive ... it helps to guide understanding and boosts confidence.'
Megan Munro, Forensic Psychology student at Leeds Trinity University College

'Very useful ... bridges the gap between Statistics textbooks and Statistics workbooks.'
Chris Lynch, Psychology student at the University of Chester

'The answer guidelines are brilliant, I wish I had had it last year.'
Tony Whalley, Psychology student at the University of Chester

'I definitely would (buy a revision guide) as I like the structure, the assessment advice and practice questions and would feel more confident knowing exactly what to revise and having something to refer to.'
Steff Copestake, Psychology student at the University of Chester

'The clarity is absolutely first rate ... These chapters will be an excellent revision guide for students as well as providing a good opportunity for novel forms of assessment in and out of class.'
Dr Deaglan Page, Queen's University, Belfast

'Do you think they will help students when revising/working towards assessment? Unreservedly, yes.'
Dr Mike Cox, Newcastle University

'The revision guide should be very helpful to students preparing for their exams.'
Dr Kun Guo, University of Lincoln

'A brilliant revision guide, very helpful for students of all levels.'
Svetoslav Georgiev, Psychology student at Anglia Ruskin University

'Develops knowledge and understanding in an easy to read manner with details on how to structure the best answers for essays and practical problems – vital for university students.'
Emily Griffiths, Psychology student at Leeds Metropolitan University

'Brilliant! Easy to read and understand – I would recommend this revision guide to every sport psychology student.'
Thomas Platt, Psychology student at Leeds Metropolitan University

Occupational Psychology

Catherine Steele
University of Leicester

Kazia Solowiej
University of Worcester

Ann Bicknell
HCPC Registered Practitioner (Occupational), FHEA

Holly Sands
SHL Group Limited, a part of CEB

Series editor:
Dominic Upton
University of Worcester

PEARSON

Harlow, England • London • New York • Boston • San Francisco • Toronto • Sydney
Auckland • Singapore • Hong Kong • Tokyo • Seoul • Taipei • New Delhi
Cape Town • São Paulo • Mexico City • Madrid • Amsterdam • Munich • Paris • Milan

Pearson Education Limited
Edinburgh Gate
Harlow CM20 2JE
United Kingdom
Tel: +44 (0)1279 623623
Web: www.pearson.com/uk

First published 2014 (print and electronic)

ISBN: 978-1-447-92168-4 (print)
      978-1-447-93089-1 (PDF)
      978-1-447-93090-7 (ePub)
      978-1-447-93088-4 (eText)

British Library Cataloguing-in-Publication Data
A catalogue record for the print edition is available from the British Library

Library of Congress Cataloging-in-Publication Data
Steele, Catherine.
Occupational psychology / Catherine Steele, Kazia Solowiej, Ann Bicknell, Holly Sands. – 1 Edition.
    pages cm – (Psychology express)
Includes bibliographical references and index.
ISBN 978-1-4479-2168-4 (pbk.)
1. Psychology, Industrial. I. Title.
HF5548.8S71884 2014
158.7 – dc23

                                                2013050540

10 9 8 7 6 5 4 3 2
17 16

Print edition typeset in 9.5/12.5pt Avenir Book by 73
Print edition printed and bound in Great Britain by Ashford Colour Press Ltd.

NOTE THAT ANY PAGE CROSS REFERENCES REFER TO THE PRINT EDITION

Contents

Companion Website

For open-access **student resources** specifically written to complement this textbook and support your learning, please visit **www.pearsoned.co.uk/psychologyexpress**

Acknowledgements

Our thanks go to all the reviewers who contributed to the development of this text, including students who participated in research and focus groups, which helped to shape the series format:

Mr Amar Cherchar, University of Northampton

Dr Almuth McDowall, University of Surrey

Dr Karin Moser, University of Roehampton, London

Dr Gail Steptoe-Warren, Coventry University

Professor Andy Tattersall, Liverpool John Moores University

Many thanks to Charlotte Winter for creating the glossary.

We are grateful to the following for permission to reproduce copyright material:

Figures

Figure 8.4 adapted from National Career Development Association (NCDA) (2007). Code of ethics., © National Career Development Association; Figure 9.1 Republished with permission of Sage Publications, Inc., from *Psychological Contracts in Organizations: Understanding Written and Unwritten Agreements*, Rousseau, D. M., 1995; permission conveyed through Copyright Clearance Center, Inc.; Figure 9.4 adapted from Chapman, A. Equity theory from http://www.businessballs.com/adamsequitytheory.htm, © JS Adams original Equity Theory concept, Alan Chapman review, code, design 1995–2014; Figure 10.1 adapted from *Organizational Change*, Senior, B., and Swailes, S., Pearson Education Limited © Barbara Senior and Stephen Swailes 2010; Figure 10.4 Reprinted from *Business Horizons*, 23(3), Waterman, R. H., Peters, T. J., and Phillips, J. R., Structure is not an organization, pp. 14–26, 1980, with permission from Elsevier; Figure 10.5 adapted from *Organisational Change*, Senior, B., and Fleming, J., Pearson Education Limited © Barbara Senior and Jocelyn Fleming 2006; Figure 10.6 adapted from *Organizational Change*, Senior, B., and Swailes, S., Pearson Education Limited © Barbara Senior and Stephen Swailes 2010.

Tables

Table 7.2 republished with permission of Sage Publications Inc Books, from *Careers in and out of Organizations*, Hall D. T., 2002; permission conveyed through Copyright Clearance Center, Inc.; Table 7.3 reproduced with the kind permission of Open University Press. All rights reserved.; Table 10.1 mission statements reproduced by kind permission of GlaxoSmithKline, Sainsbury's Supermarkets Ltd, Nike Inc., Facebook and British Heart Foundation.

Text

Extract on page 58 from ISO 9241-210:2010: Ergonomics of human-system interaction – Part 210: Human-centred design for interactive systems, © International Organization for Standardization.

In some instances we have been unable to trace the owners of copyright material, and we would appreciate any information that would enable us to do so.

Introduction

Not only is psychology one of the fastest growing subjects to study at university worldwide, it is also one of the most exciting and relevant subjects. Over the past decade the scope, breadth and importance of psychology have developed considerably. Important research work from as far afield as the UK, Europe, USA and Australia has demonstrated the exacting research base of the topic and how this can be applied to all manner of everyday issues and concerns. Being a student of psychology is an exciting experience – the study of mind and behaviour is a fascinating journey of discovery. Studying psychology at degree level brings with it new experiences, new skills and knowledge. As the Quality Assurance Agency (QAA) has stressed:

> psychology is distinctive in the rich and diverse range of attributes it develops – skills which are associated with the humanities (e.g. critical thinking and essay writing) and the sciences (hypotheses-testing and numeracy). (QAA, 2010, p. 5)

Recent evidence suggests that employers appreciate the skills and knowledge of psychology graduates, but in order to reach this pinnacle you need to develop your skills, further your knowledge and most of all successfully complete your degree to your maximum ability. The skills, knowledge and opportunities that you gain during your psychology degree will give you an edge in the employment field. The QAA stresses the high level of employment skills developed during a psychology degree:

> due to the wide range of generic skills, and the rigour with which they are taught, training in psychology is widely accepted as providing an excellent preparation for many careers. In addition to subject skills and knowledge, graduates also develop skills in communication, numeracy, teamwork, critical thinking, computing, independent learning and many others, all of which are highly valued by employers. (QAA, 2010, p. 2)

In 2010, we produced a series of books under the Psychology Express title and we are proud to note that both students and tutors have found the books extremely valuable. We appreciated that these books, representing the foundation of the Psychology undergraduate course, covered only one part of a typical course (albeit one of the most important) and that there was a need to build on the success of these and produce a series that covered the application of psychology in applied settings often covered in the latter parts of the Psychology undergraduate programme. This book is part of this new series although written and designed with the positive attributes common to all in the Psychology Express series. It is not a replacement for every single text, journal article, presentation and abstract you will read and review during the course of your degree programme. It is in no way a replacement for your lectures, seminars or additional reading. A top-rated assessment answer is likely to include considerable additional information and wider reading – and you are directed to some of these in this text. This revision guide is a conductor: directing you through the maze of your degree by providing an overview of your course, helping you formulate your ideas, and directing your reading.

Each book within Psychology Express presents a summary coverage of the key concepts, theories and research in the field, within an explicit framework of revision. The focus throughout all of the books in the series will be on how you should approach and consider your topics in relation to assessment and exams. Various features have been included to help you build up your skills and knowledge, ready for your assessments. More detail of the features can be found in the guided tour for this book on page xii.

By reading and engaging with this book, you will develop your skills and knowledge base and in this way you should excel in your studies and your associated assessments.

Psychology Express: Occupational Psychology is divided into ten chapters and your course has probably been divided up into similar sections. However we, the series authors and editor, must stress a key point: do not let the purchase, reading and engagement with the material in this text restrict your reading or your thinking. In psychology, you need to be aware of the wider literature and how it interrelates and how authors and thinkers have criticised and developed the arguments of others. So even if an essay asks you about one particular topic, you need to draw on similar issues raised in other areas of psychology. There are, of course, some similar themes that run throughout the material covered in this text, but you can learn from the other areas of psychology covered in the other texts in this series as well as from material presented elsewhere.

We hope you enjoy this text and the others in the Psychology Express series, which cover the complete knowledge base of psychology:

- *Health Psychology* (Angel Chater and Erica Cook);
- *Sport Psychology* (Paul McCarthy and Mark Allen);
- *Educational Psychology* (Penney Upton and Charlotte Taylor);
- *Occupational Psychology* (Catherine Steele, Kazia Solowiej, Anne Bicknell, Holly Sands);
- *Forensic Psychology* (Laura Caulfield and Dean Wilkinson);
- *Clinical Psychology* (Tim Jones and Phil Tyson).

This book, and the other companion volumes in this series, should cover all your study needs (there will also be further guidance on the website). It will, obviously, need to be supplemented with further reading and this text directs you towards suitable sources. Hopefully, quite a bit of what you read here you will already have come across and the text will act as a jolt to set your mind at rest – you do know the material in depth. Overall, we hope that you find this book useful and informative as a guide both for your study now and in your future as a successful psychology graduate.

Revision note

- *Use evidence based on your reading, not on anecdotes or your 'common sense'.*
- *Show the examiner you know your material in depth – use your additional reading wisely.*
- *Remember to draw on a number of different sources: there is rarely one 'correct' answer to any psychological problem.*
- *Base your conclusions on research-based evidence.*

Explore the accompanying website at www.pearsoned.co.uk/psychologyexpress
→ Prepare more effectively for exams and assignments using the answer guidelines for questions from this chapter.
→ Test your knowledge using multiple choice questions and flashcards.
→ Improve your essay skills.

Guided tour

→ Understand key concepts quickly

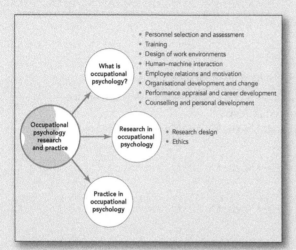

Start to plan your revision using the **Topic maps.**

Grasp **Key terms** quickly using the handy definitions. Use the flashcards online to test yourself.

Key term

Evidence-based practice: The American Psychological Association (APA) defines evidence-based practice as 'the integration of the best available research with clinical expertise in the context of patient characteristics, culture and preferences' (APA, 2005).

OPs working in practice should work from an evidence-based perspective. The APA definition above describes what this means. Within occupational psychology the word 'patient' can be replaced with the word 'client'. Evidence-based practitioners use good research evidence, evaluated using their knowledge of research methods and design, to underpin the interventions and solutions they recommend to clients. Alongside this research evidence, practitioners use their own expertise and knowledge of the client base and the industry in which they work.

→ Revise effectively

KEY STUDY

Anderson (2007): The practitioner–researcher divide revisited

In one of the more recent papers on the issue of the divide, Neil Anderson (2007) responds to previous debates. He suggests that the divide is natural and expected, and proposes a way forward in the form of a number of strategic-level bridges across the divide. These include inviting practitioner psychologists to contribute to academic courses and creating joint research groups between practitioners and researchers. The paper takes an interesting look at the historic issues that have been raised and makes considered suggestions that could help the profession move forward.

To summarise, occupational psychology consists of good research and good practice, both of which can be very varied in nature, but ultimately they always relate to the two main aims of OP:

- using psychology to improve business performance
- using psychology to improve individuals' working lives.

Quickly remind yourself of the **Key studies** using the special boxes in the text.

Test your knowledge

2.3 Give an example of how correlation could be used in occupational psychology research.

2.4 Give an example of how a qualitative approach could be used in occupational psychology research.

2.5 Why is it important to consider ethics in OP research?

2.6 What are the four domains of the BPS Code of Ethics and Standards?

Answers to these questions can be found on the companion website at: www.pearsoned.co.uk/psychologyexpress.

Prepare for upcoming exams and tests using the **Test your knowledge** and **Sample question** features.

Answer guidelines

✳ *Sample question*   *Essay*

Critically consider how the research practitioner divide in occupational psychology can be bridged.

Approaching the question

The first thing to consider is what is meant by the question. It asks you to critically consider something – the inclusion of the word 'critically' suggests that you need to weigh up the evidence and present a clear consideration of all perspectives before coming to your own conclusions.

Important points to include

● Make sure you fully explain what is meant by the divide – don't assume that the reader already knows this.

● Make sure you refer to the bridges that have already been suggested in the literature and explain how they would work and address the issue.

Make your answer stand out

To make your answer stand out you need to demonstrate a full understanding of the issues. Both sides in this debate are coming from a difference perspective – showing an appreciation of this will gain you credit. You may also have some additional suggestions for bridges alongside those that have already been considered in the literature.

Compare your responses with the **Answer guidelines** in the text and on the website.

→ **Make your answers stand out**

CRITICAL FOCUS

The BPS Code of Ethics and Conduct

The BPS Code of Ethics and Conduct applies to all psychologists working in any discipline. It is centred around four domains of responsibility:

● *Respect* – this refers to respect for confidentiality, informed consent and dignity.

● *Competence* – psychologists should practise within their own professional boundaries and be aware of ethics and ethical decision making.

● *Responsibility* – for participants and clients through protection of individuals, prevention of harm and ensuring in research that participants are thoroughly debriefed.

● *Integrity* – referring to honest and accurate reporting, appropriate professional boundaries and avoiding conflicts of interest in their work.

Use the **Critical focus** boxes to impress your examiner with your deep and critical understanding.

Make your answer stand out

To make your answer stand out you need to demonstrate a full understanding of the issues. Both sides in this debate are coming from a difference perspective – showing an appreciation of this will gain you credit. You may also have some additional suggestions for bridges alongside those that have already been considered in the literature.

Go into the exam with confidence using the handy tips to **make your answer stand out.**

1

How to use this revision guide

If you are reading this book, you are most probably preparing for a test or examination of some kind. At that point it can be helpful to read overviews of knowledge areas put together by someone else to get a different perspective and to supplement your own knowledge and understanding so far. To aid you in this, the guide was written with very clear emphasis on study skills and strategies to help you organise and reinterpret your existing knowledge as well as learn new content. A wealth of assessment advice, sample questions and associated example responses is provided so that you can check that you are on the right lines both in knowing and applying content.

The content parallels the eight knowledge domains required by the British Psychological Society (BPS) in accrediting occupational psychology (OP) programmes. The eight areas of OP are:

1 Human–machine interaction
2 Design of environments and health and safety
3 Personnel selection and assessment
4 Performance appraisal and career development
5 Counselling and personal development
6 Training
7 Employee relations and motivation
8 Organisational development and change

The BPS also requires that graduates demonstrate additional skills to uphold the status of the profession ('pure and applied') and these include: professional issues, ethical behaviour, critical evaluation skills, methodology and analysis, and an appreciation of the conventions by which theories, models and instruments are developed in occupational and organisational psychology. As this is an applied discipline, we also touch on literature from allied professions such as human resources, ergonomics and human factors, industrial relations and their sub-disciplines.

The sharp-eyed amongst you will have noticed there are ten chapters in the book, even though there are eight knowledge domains. In addition to this introductory chapter, the next, titled 'Occupational psychology research and practice', addresses the additional requirements of an applied discipline. This means that practitioners both value the scientific evidence base and understand what benefits this brings to how knowledge is created and tested through research designs and methods, in addition to the value of knowledge itself.

Each chapter is organised with a 'heads-up' revision checklist, which prepares you for what it will cover and allows you mentally to 'tick off' the subjects as you go through them. Assessment advice is provided together with examples of problem-based learning questions and worked examples of good and poor responses.

There are 'key definition' and 'critical focus' boxes in each chapter to highlight important issues in particular areas, enabling the reader to learn about the challenges of working in evidence-based practice. Use the 'test your knowledge' sections to do just that as you go through the sections; this temporary pause and reflection will help you to assimilate what you have just read and 'make it stick'.

There are some suggestions for further reading, but this should not stop you reviewing the literature yourself, using the internet to source information from credible websites such as the CIPD and HSE. Remember that the usual standards of plagiarism apply when using this information in your examinations or assessments. There is also a set of multiple-choice questions in each chapter, for you to try after you have read the chapters and the worked essay examples. Pay particular attention to the example essay and problem-based learning questions with their sections on:

- Approaching the question
- Important points to include
- Make your answer stand out

This will get you into the habit of what to think about, how to order what you write and ensuring that you include information which demonstrates those 'professional skills' of ethics and critical evaluation as well as debating relevant theories, models and research designs.

With regard to examinations, here are a few tips:

- Read the question – at least twice. Understand what you are required to do and underline key words like 'critically evaluate' if necessary. This allows you to check back on the question periodically and prevents you from drifting off at tangents.

- As with this book, marks are awarded for the structure of information as well as the volume of content. So, what you do with your information counts. Take a few minutes at the start of examinations to map out what you will cover and do not forget a brief and pointed introduction to signpost the reader. At the end, ensure you conclude with a robust statement that flows logically from the information you have presented.

- Examiners are not trying to 'catch you out' or trick you. Be confident and say something intelligent in response the question – you probably know more than you think.

- Finally, don't panic. You might like to consolidate large amounts of written revision content onto one sheet of A4 as a 'mind map' a couple of days before the exam. You could have one piece of paper for each subject area, which triggers your memory and could be applied to a range of questions in that domain.
- Very best wishes and good luck on the day!

Notes

Notes

2

Occupational psychology research and practice

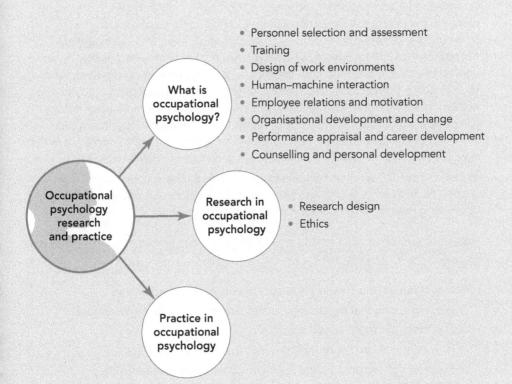

- **Occupational psychology research and practice**

- **What is occupational psychology?**
  - Personnel selection and assessment
  - Training
  - Design of work environments
  - Human–machine interaction
  - Employee relations and motivation
  - Organisational development and change
  - Performance appraisal and career development
  - Counselling and personal development

- **Research in occupational psychology**
  - Research design
  - Ethics

- **Practice in occupational psychology**

A printable version of this topic map is available from
www.pearsoned.co.uk/psychologyexpress

Introduction

Occupational psychology is one of the largest areas of practising psychology and represents the second largest division of the British Psychological Society (behind Clinical Psychology). A variety of terms are used to apply to this discipline and at first this may appear confusing. In the United Kingdom the term 'occupational psychology' is used to refer to psychology applied to the workplace and business. In the United States this is called industrial/organisational or I/O psychology. It is also referred to as business psychology, work psychology and organisational psychology, sometimes interchangeably. Throughout this text the term 'occupational psychology' (OP) will be used. There are also other closely related fields such as organisational development (OD), human resources management (HRM), management consultancy, coaching and ergonomics.

As a discipline, occupational psychology has grown rapidly in recent years in both research and practice. Occupational psychologists apply psychological theory to business and the world of work and it is this application that distinguishes occupational psychology from the closely related fields mentioned above. As an applied area, OP utilises the core areas of psychology by making them relevant to organisations. For example, theories about groups from social psychology can be applied to team performance and composition. Knowledge from biopsychology can be applied to maximise the performance of shift workers. Personality and theories of individual differences can be used to ensure the right people are in the right job roles both at the recruitment stage and in career development.

In this chapter OP will first be defined and outlined. The second part of the chapter focuses on research and practice and considers one of the key debates concerning how these two areas can be brought together.

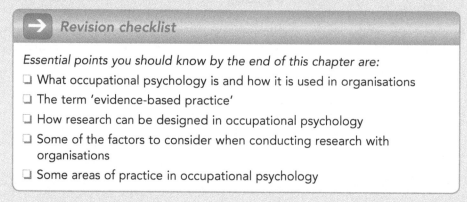

→ *Revision checklist*

Essential points you should know by the end of this chapter are:
- ❏ What occupational psychology is and how it is used in organisations
- ❏ The term 'evidence-based practice'
- ❏ How research can be designed in occupational psychology
- ❏ Some of the factors to consider when conducting research with organisations
- ❏ Some areas of practice in occupational psychology

Assessment advice

Typical assessments in this area are likely to be discussion or opinion based. For example, an exam question might ask you to 'Critically discuss the use of evidence-based practice within occupational psychology.' With a question like this it is important to remember that any statements you make must be supported with evidence. There are a number of peer-reviewed papers and even special editions of journals dedicated to this very topic. Stronger answers will weigh up the evidence effectively and come to a clear conclusion. Answers to this sort of question could take quite a broad perspective by commenting on the training route and career paths of occupational psychologists and how well evidence-based practice is embedded in those processes.

Sample question

Could you answer this question? Below is a typical essay question that could arise on this topic.

✱ *Sample question*   **Essay**

Critically consider how the research–practitioner divide in occupational psychology can be bridged.

Guidelines on answering this question are included at the end of this chapter, whilst guidance on tackling other exam questions can be found on the companion website at **www.pearsoned.co.uk/psychologyexpress**

Further reading	
Topic	*Key reading*
Occupational psychology in the United Kingdom	http://dop.bps.org.uk
Occupational (or I/O) psychology in the United States	http://www.siop.org
Careers in occupational psychology	http://dop.bps.org.uk/dop/public/careers-qualifications/careers-qualifications_home.cfm#training

What is occupational psychology?

As stated above, occupational psychology is about applying the theories of psychology to the workplace. Historically, large developments took place in the twentieth century. During the First World War, the Health and Munitions Workers Committee and the Industrial Health Research Board were established to investigate the effect of fatigue on the efficiency of workers. In 1921 Myers founded the National Institute of Industrial Psychology, whose aim was to 'promote and encourage the application of the science of psychology and physiology to commerce and industry' (Shimmin & Wallis, 1994, p. 4). In the Second World War methods of recruitment and selection in the military were transformed and psychological assessments were introduced on a large scale. Postwar these methods were established within the civil service and OP continued to grow and expand into other areas of workplace efficiency.

Occupational psychologists generally have two main aims. First, they are often employed or consulted by organisations to improve business performance in some way. This might be through improving the efficiency of processes, increasing staff motivation or even redesigning the organisational structure. The second aim (and the two are often linked) is to improve the working lives of individuals. This might be done through ensuring that workplaces are designed to be comfortable and to allow the individual to do their job well, it might be through advising on career choice, or it might be working on stress management and work–life balance. Within the United Kingdom it is currently accepted that there are eight areas of OP and these are outlined in more detail below.

1 Personnel selection and assessment

One of the most common areas of work for occupational psychologists is in selection and assessment. This includes conducting job analyses, designing recruitment processes, using psychometric tests and even devising assessment processes for development and redundancy programmes. See Chapter 3 for more information on this area.

2 Training

Occupational psychologists use theories about human learning to design workplace training. Training needs analysis can be conducted to identify any areas where training is needed, and psychologists also use their skills to advise organisations on how to evaluate training and maximise return on investment (ROI). See Chapter 4.

3 Design of work environments

One of the lesser-known areas of occupational psychology, design of work environments is related to health and safety and also to environmental psychology. Specialists in this area use their knowledge to advise organisations on office design and work station analysis and even look at issues such as toxic building syndrome and the impact this has on wellbeing at work. Stress management may also be covered here. See Chapters 5 and 10.

4 Human–machine interaction

This is another of the less well-known areas and has close links with engineering psychology and ergonomics. Human–machine interaction refers to the way in which we use equipment in the workplace and uses psychological knowledge of perception and cognitive processes in the design of this. For example, in the design of aeroplane cockpits or nuclear power stations, the specialist would ensure that the occurrence of human error was minimised. See Chapter 4.

5 Employee relations and motivation

Motivation is one of the most studied topics in OP – there are hundreds of thousands of papers that address this topic. Motivating staff is a key factor for organisations and an issue on which many managers seek advice and support. A related area is employee relations – this could refer to trade union involvement or the development of the psychological contract. Theories of leadership would also be considered here along with development of leadership training and guidance. See Chapters 8 and 11.

6 Organisational development and change

There are many theories of organisational development (OD) and change that are studied in business; however, psychology has a unique contribution to make here in understanding the human implications of change. This might relate to understanding of identity and group work from social psychology, and how change may affect this. It may be concerned with how change is communicated in organisations and the impact this has on individuals. See Chapter 9.

7 Performance appraisal and career development

Most organisations will conduct an annual performance appraisal with their staff. Psychology can contribute here by ensuring these are run effectively and by implementing new processes such as 360 degree feedback. Theories of personality and individual differences can be applied to aid career development and career guidance, and make sure that individuals are in roles and organisations where they will flourish. See Chapter 8.

8 Counselling and personal development

The final one of the eight areas relates to workplace counselling and personal development. Reasons for counselling at work may relate to bullying, harassment, stress or even redundancy or outplacement work. One of the fastest-growing areas of personal development within the workplace is coaching and psychology can be used to ensure that workplace coaching is evidence based and grounded in psychological theory. See Chapter 7.

This section has provided an overview of occupational psychology and the areas in which occupational psychologists work and apply their knowledge. The remainder of this book is structured around these areas and more detailed information about each of them can be found throughout the book. In addition there are separate chapters on leadership and workplace wellbeing as these are large areas and deserve full consideration. The next section of this chapter focuses on research in occupational psychology, particularly research methods, and it considers some of the challenges of conducting research in this area.

Test your knowledge

2.1 What are the eight areas of occupational psychology?

2.2 What are the two main aims of occupational psychology?

Answers to these questions can be found on the companion website at: **www.pearsoned.co.uk/psychologyexpress.**

Further reading

Topic	Key reading
Occupational psychology	Millward, L. (2005). *Understanding occupational and organizational psychology.* London: Sage.
History of occupational psychology	Shimmin, S., & Wallis, D. (1994). *Fifty years of occupational psychology in Britain.* Leicester: British Psychological Society.

Research in occupational psychology

Occupational psychology is an evidence-based discipline; therefore the work of all OPs should be underpinned by research. OP borrows research findings from all areas of psychology to inform its discipline: for example, classic behaviourist studies can be used to inform some of the approaches taken to training in organisations and some of the classic social psychology studies inform how we look at groups and teams at work. Building on classic works, OP research is vast and there are a large number of peer-reviewed journals dedicated to it – for example, the *Journal of Occupational and Organizational Psychology* published by the BPS. This section will look first at the many types of research design in this area and then at the role of ethics in OP research.

Research design

One of the difficulties with research in this area is how to design it. As OP is an applied field, the ideal way to conduct research would be in the field, working with real organisations and employees. However, there are a number of challenges with conducting research in this way. This section will look first at the challenges involved in the design of research and then at the different methodologies that are commonly used in this area.

One of the criticisms of psychological research in general is that much of it has been conducted with white, middle-class (and classically male) student samples. Some research in OP could also be subject to this same criticism. However, there is also a wide range of research that has been conducted within organisations and with working adults. Increasingly, as the world of work has been globalised, research is emerging that addresses this by taking a cross-cultural approach.

Conducting research with organisations is challenging. First, the organisation must be identified and access negotiated. At this point the needs of the researcher and the organisation need to be met and agreed. Organisations are rapidly changing environments and research can sometimes take a long time, during which the environment may change – this makes any kind of experimental control difficult.

Research in OP has utilised quantitative and qualitative methods. Quantitative approaches include correlational studies and regression analysis, where the research is looking for relationships between variables and to predict the value of one variable based on the value of another. For example, in recruitment researchers are interested in how well performance on a selection test predicts workplace performance. Tests of difference may also be used, utilising statistical analyses such as ANOVA and MANOVA. For example, an organisation may want to know how effective a training course has been for its employees, so knowledge of the subject matter could be measured before, during and after the training to see what employees have learnt. Factor analysis is another commonly used technique in OP research, particularly in the development of psychometric tests. For example, when developing a new occupational measure, factor analysis is used to examine the structure of the test and the variables being measured. A number of meta-analyses have also been conducted that aim to summarise large bodies of work: for example, Schmidt and Hunter (1998) examined 85 years of research into selection methods using this approach.

Qualitative methods have also been applied – the use of focus groups and interviews is common in OP. They can be used to explore topics in more depth: for example, story techniques can be used to consider an individual's career development over their lifespan. Diary studies can be used to examine experience of stress, while thematic or discourse analysis can be used to explore organisational culture.

Research in OP can be designed in a variety of ways depending on the topic under investigation. As with all psychological research involving human beings, ethical considerations must be adhered to and the following section examines this in more detail.

Ethics

All psychologists should be researching and practising ethically. Ethics refer to a code of conduct or moral principles common to a group of individuals, in this case to psychologists. OP researchers will normally be affiliated to a university

11

and any research proposed will be subject to the scrutiny of the university's board of ethics – the work will be required to gain their approval before the research can commence. When working with certain organisations or research funding bodies, such as the NHS, these may also have their own ethical guidelines. Psychologists can refer to the code of ethics and conduct produced by the British Psychological Society, more details of which can be found in the box below.

CRITICAL FOCUS

The BPS Code of Ethics and Conduct

The BPS Code of Ethics and Conduct applies to all psychologists working in any discipline. It is centred around four domains of responsibility:

- *Respect* – this refers to respect for confidentiality, informed consent and dignity.
- *Competence* – psychologists should practise within their own professional boundaries and be aware of ethics and ethical decision making.
- *Responsibility* – for participants and clients through protection of individuals, prevention of harm and ensuring in research that participants are thoroughly debriefed.
- *Integrity* – referring to honest and accurate reporting, appropriate professional boundaries and avoiding conflicts of interest in their work.

Further reading

Topic	Key reading
Research approaches in occupational psychology	Rogelberg, S. J. (2004). *Handbook of research methods in industrial organisational psychology.* Oxford: Blackwell.
Qualitative research in occupational psychology	Symon, G., & Cassell, C. (2012). *Qualitative organisational research: Core methods and current challenges.* London: Sage.
Ethics in psychology	http://www.bps.org.uk/what-we-do/ethics-standards/ethics-standards

Test your knowledge

2.3 Give an example of how correlation could be used in occupational psychology research.

2.4 Give an example of how a qualitative approach could be used in occupational psychology research.

2.5 Why is it important to consider ethics in OP research?

2.6 What are the four domains of the BPS Code of Ethics and Standards?

Answers to these questions can be found on the companion website at: www.pearsoned.co.uk/psychologyexpress.

Practice in occupational psychology

One of the key questions from both undergraduate and postgraduate students in occupational psychology is 'What do occupational psychologists do?' The answer is: it really varies! A lot of OPs work as independent consultants, meaning that they work for themselves and undertake work for a variety of organisations. Independent consultants may specialise in one particular area of OP or they may work across several areas. There are a number of large consultancy firms that employ occupational psychologists: for example, SHL, Pearn Kandola and Kasien, all based in the United Kingdom. Consultants are employed in these organisations and are then allocated to certain client projects depending on their expertise and experience. Some OPs will be employed by organisations like Sainsbury's, the National Police Improvement Agency and British Airways. Working in house for an organisation, these psychologists provide specialist services, often focusing on recruitment and retention.

To qualify as an occupational psychologist individuals need to:

● complete an undergraduate degree in psychology that is accredited by the BPS

● complete an MSc in Occupational Psychology accredited by the BPS, normally 1 year full time or 2 years part time

● complete the Qualification in Occupational Psychology – a BPS qualification that takes at least 2 years to complete. The QOccPsy involves writing up your experience of supervised practice in different areas of psychology.

Once these stages have been completed, it is possible to apply for chartered membership of the BPS and to apply to the Health Professions Council (HPC) as a practitioner psychologist and occupational psychologist.

Key term

Evidence-based practice: The American Psychological Association (APA) defines evidence-based practice as 'the integration of the best available research with clinical expertise in the context of patient characteristics, culture and preferences' (APA, 2005).

OPs working in practice should work from an evidence-based perspective. The APA definition above describes what this means. Within occupational psychology the word 'patient' can be replaced with the word 'client'. Evidence-based practitioners use good research evidence, evaluated using their knowledge of research methods and design, to underpin the interventions and solutions they recommend to clients. Alongside this research evidence, practitioners use their own expertise and knowledge of the client base and the industry in which they work.

There has been an ongoing debate within the industry about the divide between practitioners and researchers in psychology. A number of criticisms have been made which suggest that academics and practitioners do not work closely enough together. The criticism made of the researchers is that they research topics that are not of interest to practitioner psychologists and their clients. The practitioners have

▶

been accused of not using the available research evidence to underpin their work or to evaluate fully the approach they take. This is a continuing issue that has been debated at a number of recent conferences, nationally and internationally.

KEY STUDY

Anderson (2007): The practitioner–researcher divide revisited

In one of the more recent papers on the issue of the divide, Neil Anderson (2007) responds to previous debates. He suggests that the divide is natural and expected, and proposes a way forward in the form of a number of strategic-level bridges across the divide. These include inviting practitioner psychologists to contribute to academic courses and creating joint research groups between practitioners and researchers. The paper takes an interesting look at the historic issues that have been raised and makes considered suggestions that could help the profession move forward.

To summarise, occupational psychology consists of good research and good practice, both of which can be very varied in nature, but ultimately they always relate to the two main aims of OP:

- using psychology to improve business performance
- using psychology to improve individuals' working lives.

Further reading

Topic	Key reading
The Qualification in Occupational Psychology	http://www.bps.org.uk/careers-education-training/society-qualifications/occupational-psychology/occupational-psychology

Test your knowledge

2.7 What do we mean by evidence-based practice?

2.8 How do you qualify as an occupational psychologist?

2.9 What do we mean by the divide in occupational psychology?

Answers to these questions can be found on the companion website at: **www.pearsoned.co.uk/psychologyexpress.**

Chapter summary – pulling it all together

→ Can you tick all the points from the revision checklist at the beginning of this chapter?

→ Attempt the sample question from the beginning of this chapter using the answer guidelines below.

→ Go to the companion website at www.pearsoned.co.uk/psychologyexpress to access more revision support online, including interactive quizzes, flashcards, You be the marker exercises as well as answer guidance for the Test your knowledge and Sample questions from this chapter.

Answer guidelines

 Sample question   **Essay**

> Critically consider how the research–practitioner divide in occupational psychology can be bridged.

Approaching the question

The first thing to consider is what is meant by the question. It asks you to critically consider something – the inclusion of the word 'critically' suggests that you need to weigh up the evidence and present a clear consideration of all perspectives before coming to your own conclusions.

Important points to include

- Make sure you fully explain what is meant by the divide – don't assume that the reader already knows this.
- Make sure you refer to the bridges that have already been suggested in the literature and explain how they would work and address the issue.

Make your answer stand out

To make your answer stand out you need to demonstrate a full understanding of the issues. Both sides in this debate are coming from a difference perspective – showing an appreciation of this will gain you credit. You may also have some additional suggestions for bridges alongside those that have already been considered in the literature.

Further reading

Arnold, J., Randall, R., Patterson, F., & Silvester, J. (2010). *Work psychology: Understanding human behaviour in the workplace*. London: Prentice Hall.

Warr, P (2002). *Psychology at work*. London: Penguin.

Zibarras, L., & Lewis, R. (2012). *Occupational psychology: Integrating theory and practice*. London: Sage.

Explore the accompanying website at www.pearsoned.co.uk/psychologyexpress

→ Prepare more effectively for exams and assignments using the answer guidelines for questions from this chapter.

→ Test your knowledge using multiple choice questions and flashcards.

→ Improve your essay skills by exploring the You be the marker exercises.

Notes

Personnel selection and assessment

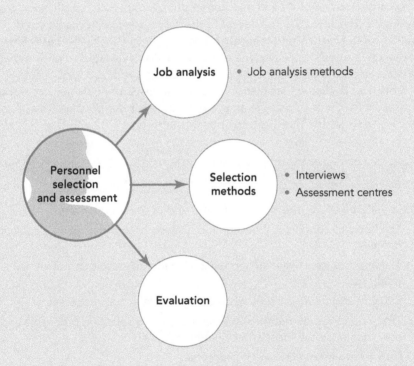

Job analysis
- Job analysis methods

Personnel selection and assessment

Selection methods
- Interviews
- Assessment centres

Evaluation

A printable version of this topic map is available from
www.pearsoned.co.uk/psychologyexpress

Introduction

Selecting the right people for an organisation is critical for its success. Schmidt, Gast-Rosenberg, and Hunter (1980) estimated that the difference in value between a poor and a good manager is between £12,000 and £42,000. The cost of recruiting the wrong candidate into a role can run into hundreds of thousands of pounds. Occupational psychologists help organisations by using their knowledge of human behaviour, research methods and business to design robust selection processes that ensure the right person gets selected. They start by analysing the job vacancies that organisations need to fill, then they design an appropriate selection process to make sure the right person is found for those vacancies.

There are three key components to selection and assessment. The first is job analysis – this is the starting point, where the jobs under consideration need to be considered carefully and a job description and person specification are developed. The second is the design of the actual selection process – this involves using practical and theoretical knowledge to choose the best methods for the job in question. Finally, the process must be evaluated to ensure that it has achieved the desired results and successfully predicted employee performance. Evaluation enables us, as psychologists, to apply our knowledge of research methods to provide an evidence base for our practice. This chapter will cover each of the three key components in turn.

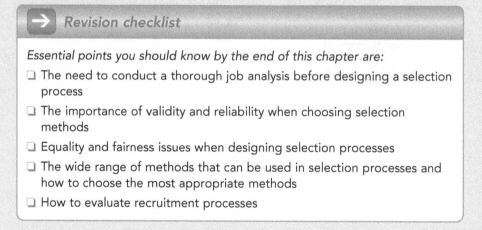

→ Revision checklist

Essential points you should know by the end of this chapter are:
- ❏ The need to conduct a thorough job analysis before designing a selection process
- ❏ The importance of validity and reliability when choosing selection methods
- ❏ Equality and fairness issues when designing selection processes
- ❏ The wide range of methods that can be used in selection processes and how to choose the most appropriate methods
- ❏ How to evaluate recruitment processes

Assessment advice

Typical assessments in this area are likely to be based on a case study and require you to design a selection procedure for a particular job role. The key thing to remember here is to provide a balance of both academic and practical considerations in your response. If you are provided with a job description and person specification, you will need to base your response on these. If not, you may also be required to conduct a job analysis to create your own.

The key point to remember about selection is that you are trying to predict future behaviour and no selection process will be 100 per cent perfect! Therefore you need to use your knowledge of concepts like reliability and validity to design the best possible recruitment process for the job in question and within budgetary constraints. You will need a good knowledge of the range of assessments available, how they differ and how they can be combined. You will also need to be able to make sensible suggestions about how to evaluate the process you design. How will you be able to demonstrate to your client that it is adding value?

Sample question

Could you answer this question? Below is a typical problem question that could arise on this topic.

 Sample question   *Problem-based learning*

You have been asked to conduct a job analysis for the role of a maths lecturer at your university. Outline the methods you would use and provide a clear justification for your chosen approach.

Guidelines on answering this question are included at the end of this chapter, whilst guidance on tackling other exam questions can be found on the companion website at **www.pearsoned.co.uk/psychologyexpress**

Job analysis

The aim of job analysis is to produce a job description and person specification upon which the rest of the selection process can be built. The job description should outline all of the activities that the job holder is required to do. It may also have details about salary or grade for the position and how the position fits into an organisational structure. The second aim is to develop a person specification – this document outlines the personal characteristics, knowledge, skills and attributes (KSAs) that the job holder should possess. Both of these documents form an important part of the selection and assessment process, as they provide a baseline against which candidates can be measured.

Job analysis can also be used for other human resources issues, such as identifying training needs, performance management and career planning. It is a key activity but one that is often overlooked.

Job analysis methods

There are a number of different ways to approach the job analysis. The method used will depend on a variety of factors including:

- *Job level* (e.g. choosing a long and expensive method for a junior, low-paid role would not be cost effective)
- *Job type* (e.g. choosing an observational method for the job analysis of a brain surgeon would be too simplistic)
- *Expertise of the analyst* (e.g. using a method that you have never used before and have not had a chance to trial would probably not be effective).

One of the most straightforward ways to conduct a job analysis is simply to observe the current job holder and see what they are doing. This is only suitable for roles where it is clear to see what the job holder is doing. For example, observing a cleaner would enable you to ascertain how long they spent on certain tasks and what they did in each room. However, when observing you need to have a structured method of note taking; you also need to decide in advance how long you will observe for and be aware of the Hawthorne effect.

Alternatively, you might conduct an interview with a job holder to ask specific questions about their job role. Diaries may also be used, but response rates can be low and you are relying on job holders to record information accurately. Other methods include the critical incident technique (Flanagan, 1954), where job holders are asked to recall incidents of exceptionally good or poor performance, focus groups, videoing job incumbents and open-ended questionnaires, such as the Position Analysis Questionnaire (McCormick, Jeanneret, & Mechan, 1972).

All of these methods have advantages and disadvantages and it is the role of the psychologist to decide upon the best approach for the job under consideration.

Test your knowledge

3.1 What are the aims of job analysis?

3.2 How would job level affect the method of job analysis used?

3.3 Name a job where observation would be a suitable method of job analysis. Why did you choose that job?

3.4 Name a job where observation would not be a suitable method of job analysis. Why not?

Answers to these questions can be found on the companion website at: **www.pearsoned.co.uk/psychologyexpress**.

Further reading

Topic	Key reading
Job analysis methods	Cook, M. (2009). *Personnel selection: Adding value through people*. London: Wiley.

Selection methods

Once the job analysis has been conducted, the resulting job description and person specification can be used to aid the design of the selection process. Just as in job analysis, a wide range of methods can be used for selection and it is the occupational psychologist's role to decide which method is best suited to each particular job vacancy. There are a number of factors involved in this decision-making process including:

- *Reliability of method* – is the chosen method a reliable way of analysing the KSAs under consideration?
- *Validity of methods* – does the chosen method measure what it is supposed to measure?
- *Utility analysis* – is the chosen method a cost-effective and practical strategy for the job under consideration?

The following section will provide an overview of some of the more common methods of selection.

Interviews

Almost all selection processes involve an interview of some kind. Interviews have been described as a conversation with a purpose (Searle, 2003) and they are by far the most common method used to recruit a person into a job role. It is important to be aware that there are many different ways of conducting an interview and the type of interview used has a big impact on its reliability in a selection process. One of the most common distinctions between interviews is whether they are structured or unstructured. A structured interview occurs when the interviewers have a list of questions that have been decided in advance of the interview and every candidate gets asked exactly the same questions. Structured interviews are much more reliable than unstructured, as they provide an objective way to make comparisons between candidates. One type of structured interview is the competency-based interview.

Key term

Competency-based interview: Competency-based interviews have become very popular in the last 5–10 years. They are a form of structured interview where the questions are based on a predetermined set of competencies that have been shown to predict performance on the job. Competency-based interview questions ask the candidates to provide specific examples of when they have displayed certain competencies. For example, a typical question could be: 'Give me an example of when you worked as part of team.' Guidance on answering competency-based interviews tends to focus on a method known as STAR (situation, task, action, result).

Psychometric tests

Psychometric test: A psychometric test is a set of questions which are standardised and objective, and enable differentiation between people based on their scores. Psychometric test development is a sophisticated and time-consuming process. Developers have to make sure the tests are reliable and valid, and often they will also collect large data sets to provide norm groups for comparison. There are two main types of psychometric test: ability and personality.

One of the methods with the highest predictive validity in selection processes is the cognitive ability test. It has long been known that general ability predicts performance in certain types of job (Ghiselli, 1966; Hunter & Hunter, 1984). There are a wide range of psychometric tests available for use within selection processes, from general ability tests to very specific tests such as clerical aptitude tests. The British Psychological Society regulates the use of psychometric tests in occupational psychology by making it compulsory for those who buy and use tests to be trained.

A lot of people involved in selection like to use psychometric tests as they provide what appears to be an objective way of distinguishing between people. The results from ability tests are clear and it is simple to see which candidates performed the best. However, they are not without problems. One of the criticisms of psychometric tests is that they sometimes appear to discriminate against certain groups. For example, if the questions contained within the test are based on Western cultures then it would not be appropriate for a candidate who is not familiar with that culture to take the test. Ability tests are often used at the start of selection processes, to screen out candidates, therefore it is vital to make sure that the tests being used have been shown to predict performance for the job in question and that they do not discriminate against any demographic groups.

The other type of psychometric tests used within selection processes are personality measures. Again there are a wide variety of personality measures available, all taking a slightly different perspective on what personality is. Some, for example, measure personality type, such as the Myers–Briggs Type indicator; others are based on Cattell's trait personality theory – for example, the 16PF. More recently, measures of emotional intelligence have become popular and some of these have been incorporated into selection processes.

Using personality measures in selection

It has been said that personality measures should never be used as a deciding factor in a selection process. There is no such thing as a good or bad personality; instead these measures tell us something about the candidate's behavioural preferences. As such the reports from these measures can be used to inform interview structures. If there is something in the

▶

report that a recruiter wishes to understand more about, it might be appropriate to ask the candidate about it in the interview (as long as they have seen the report first). Alternatively, the personality report might be used to structure the successful candidate's development within the role once they have been selected. Some recruiters will try to use personality measures as part of selection decision making; however, the research on this suggests that personality measures are not a good predictor of performance (Barrick & Mount, 1991).

In summary, psychometric tests are a good supplement to a recruitment process. Ability tests can be used in the initial stages of a process to screen out candidates who do not reach a certain level and personality tests can be used at later stages to find out more about a person.

Further reading

Topic	Key reading
BPS psychometric test training courses	www.psyctesting.org.uk
Psychometric test development	Kline, P. (2004). *The handbook of psychological testing.* London: Routledge.
Using personality measures in selection	Barrick, M. R., & Mount, M. K. (1991). The big five personality dimensions and job performance: A meta analysis. *Journal of Applied Psychology,* 44, 1–26.

Assessment centres

Assessment centres are a combination technique where a range of selection methods are used together. The candidates come together for one or two days and are required to take part in a number of exercises: for example, a group activity, an interview, a presentation, a role play and maybe to take some psychometric tests. At the assessment centre the candidates' performance will be observed by a number of different people. At the end of the centre those assessors will sit down together and engage in something called a wash-up. This is where the performance of the candidates is compared and selection decisions are made.

Assessment centres are one of the most expensive selection methods available because of the time taken to complete them and the number of people involved. Therefore this is something to consider when deciding to use this approach to selection.

KEY STUDY

Schmidt & Hunter (1998): The validity and utility of selection methods in personnel psychology

Schmidt and Hunter's paper uses meta-analysis to highlight the validity of 19 different selection methods and the validity of combinations of these methods. General mental ability tests combined with work sample tests or structured interviews provided the highest-validity coefficients (0.63).

Test your knowledge

3.5 What is the difference between a structured and an unstructured interview?

3.6 Give an example of a competency-based interview question.

3.7 What is a psychometric test?

3.8 Can personality measures be used as part of a selection process, and if so, how?

3.9 What is a wash-up session?

Answers to these questions can be found on the companion website at: www.pearsoned.co.uk/psychologyexpress.

Evaluation

One of the key tasks of occupational psychologists is to be able to evaluate the work that they do. In terms of selection and assessment, we must be able to demonstrate via evaluation that the selection processes we recommend and use actually work: in other words, that they do predict the job performance of candidates. Using our knowledge of research design and research methods, we can design straightforward evaluation processes that demonstrate this for our clients.

However, the quality of the evaluation depends on how well the selection process was designed in the first place. Ideally, the criterion for evaluation should have been decided at the start. Typical criteria for evaluation of selection processes include: supervisor ratings, training performance or, in certain roles, customer response or sales figures. Within selection and performance measurement more generally there is something known as the criterion problem. This refers to the fact that a lot of the criteria are subject to measurement bias. For example, supervisor ratings can be subjective depending on whether the supervisor likes the person or not. Sometimes organisations do not keep records of such things, which makes evaluation difficult because the data required are simply not available.

Assuming that the criterion has been defined at the outset and accurate records of the criterion measurement exist, we can evaluate a programme by comparing the candidates' scores from the selection process to their scores on the criterion measure. We just need to conduct a correlation or a regression analysis depending on the number of variables we have. The outcome of the analysis will show us how well our process is predicting performance (an indication of criterion validity). However, there is one final problem to be aware of: range restrictions.

Key term

Range restriction: When evaluating a selection process, we don't have all the data we need. This is because not everyone who sat the selection process gets taken on by the organisation. Therefore we cannot possibly tell how the candidates who performed badly in the section process would have performed in the job.

To summarise, it is important to evaluate any selection process, particularly if the process is going to be used again. Evaluation can be time consuming and is not always a straightforward process. However, without it we have no way of knowing if our selection processes are effective.

Test your knowledge

3.10 What types of measures do we use to evaluate selection processes?

3.11 What analyses are used to evaluate selection processes?

3.12 Describe the two main problems with evaluating selection processes.

Answers to these questions can be found on the companion website at: www.pearsoned.co.uk/psychologyexpress.

Chapter summary – pulling it all together

→ Can you tick all the points from the revision checklist at the beginning of this chapter?

→ Attempt the sample question from the beginning of this chapter using the answer guidelines below.

→ Go to the companion website at www.pearsoned.co.uk/psychologyexpress to access more revision support online, including interactive quizzes, flashcards, You be the marker exercises as well as answer guidance for the Test your knowledge and Sample questions from this chapter.

Answer guidelines

 Sample question   *Problem-based learning*

You have been asked to conduct a job analysis for the role of a maths lecturer at your university. Outline the methods you would use and provide a clear justification for your chosen approach.

Approaching the question

The first thing to consider is what method you are going to use to conduct your job analysis. You will need to familiarise yourself with the range of approaches available and be clear about what information you need from the job analysis.

Important points to include

There is no right or wrong method to use, but whatever method you choose you will need to give a theoretically and practically based justification for your choice. For example, if you choose to use observation, you will need to make sure you have access to lecturers. You will also need to think about how long you will need to observe them for, and how many lecturers you will observe. Also, what does the literature say about observation as a method of job analysis? Is it suitable for this type of role?

Make your answer stand out

To make your answer stand out, you need to demonstrate an ability to use an evidence base and practical, business knowledge for your decisions. All applied psychologists need to show that they are able to base their recommendations on good science, but also demonstrate an awareness of the client they are working with, in this case a university. In this answer you are likely to make comments about the cost of job analysis, as you are working with a public sector organisation and budgets may be constrained.

Further reading

Cook, M. (2009). *Personnel selection: Adding value through people*. London: Wiley.

Searle, R. H. (2003). *Selection and assessment: A critical text*. Basingstoke: Palgrave Macmillan.

Explore the accompanying website at www.pearsoned.co.uk/psychologyexpress
→ Prepare more effectively for exams and assignments using the answer guidelines for questions from this chapter.
→ Test your knowledge using multiple choice questions and flashcards.
→ Improve your essay skills by exploring the You be the marker exercises.

Notes

Notes

Notes

4

Training

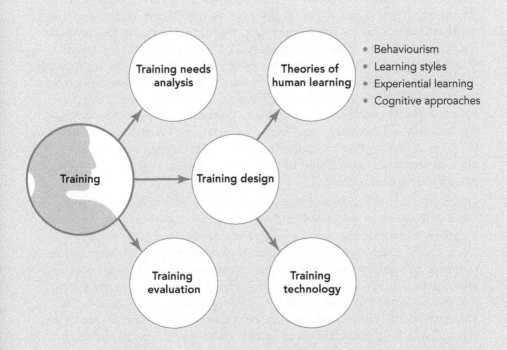

- Behaviourism
- Learning styles
- Experiential learning
- Cognitive approaches

A printable version of this topic map is available from
www.pearsoned.co.uk/psychologyexpress

Introduction

Training has been defined as 'the systematic acquisition of skills, rules, concepts or attitudes that result in improved performance in another environment' (Goldstein & Ford, 2002, p. 7). It involves learning and the application of that learning to enhance individual and organisational performance. Workplace training has changed from being mainly instruction based, where the learning takes place in a classroom and the learners are seen as passive receivers of knowledge, to something more dynamic. There are numerous training techniques available to organisations and the development of technology means that the way training can be delivered is constantly evolving.

Recent schools of thought see learners as active participants rather than passive receivers of knowledge. This in turn has influenced the role of the trainers, who are now seen as there to facilitate knowledge acquisition rather than simply to teach. Work-related training takes many forms. Traditional education programmes such as degree courses in medicine, or professional qualifications in subjects like accountancy, are forms of training that provide the skills required to enter into a profession. Similarly, National Vocational Qualifications (NVQs) can be taken in a wide range of topic areas (for example, hairdressing and catering) and like other educational approaches they provide the learners with a transportable qualification. Other forms of training may include in-house courses, for example on health and safety processes; and informal on-the-job training, also known as 'sitting with Nellie'. Coaching is a form of training that has grown in popularity in recent years, while management training is offered by many organisations, as are various forms of computer-based training.

Organisations in the United Kingdom spend billions of pounds on training every year and there are awards such as Investors in People for organisations that show a commitment to the training and development of their staff. Occupational psychologists are well placed to advise organisations and make sure that they get a good return on that investment. You will remember from your course that we do this in three main ways. First, we need to make sure that there is a need for training and then identify exactly what that need is. This is called a training needs analysis and is covered in the first section of this chapter, where we consider how to identify training needs on an individual and organisational level. Secondly, using the results of the training needs analysis, we can apply our knowledge of how adults learn and our awareness of different methods of training design to ensure that training programmes maximise learning capacity and retention. These factors are all revised in the second section of this chapter on training design. Here, human learning, training techniques and transfer of training to the workplace are also considered. Finally we can use our research methods skills to design effective training evaluations that examine the effectiveness of the training and enable organisations to assess return on investment. This is considered in the final section of this chapter, which looks at training evaluation in detail and asks: how can we ensure that a training programme has been successful? It will look at the criteria for success and the methods available for training evaluation.

This staged approach to training is called the systems approach (McGhee & Thayer, 1961) and views training as a process linked to other organisational systems. For example, the organisation's recruitment system will have a direct link to the training and development system; and the skills and knowledge a candidate comes into an organisation with have a direct impact on the training they need once they are there, so the two systems interact.

As you read through this chapter, it should remind you of what you have already learnt on your course and provide you with additional areas to consider and question.

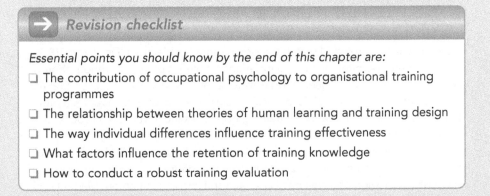

→ Revision checklist

Essential points you should know by the end of this chapter are:

- ❏ The contribution of occupational psychology to organisational training programmes
- ❏ The relationship between theories of human learning and training design
- ❏ The way individual differences influence training effectiveness
- ❏ What factors influence the retention of training knowledge
- ❏ How to conduct a robust training evaluation

Assessment advice

Typical assessments in this area will focus on the application of psychological principles and theory to the practice of training and learning within organisations. This is the unique contribution that is made by occupational psychologists. Students need to understand and be able to evidence the way in which psychological research contributes to this area of work and how it provides a unique contribution over and above that of management studies and human resource professionals. Students should use their critical thinking and research methodology skills to ensure an evidence-based approach is taken to assessments in this area. Good students will demonstrate an ability to apply research to practice and recognise the way in which research findings may need to be adapted or modified to ensure practical success.

Sample question

Could you answer this question? Below is a typical essay question that could arise on this topic.

Sample question | **Essay**

Critically evaluate the contribution of theories of knowledge acquisition to the design and practice of training.

Guidelines on answering this question are included at the end of this chapter, whilst guidance on tackling other exam questions can be found on the companion website at **www.pearsoned.co.uk/psychologyexpress**

Training needs analysis

As outlined above, training and learning expenditure can represent a significant cost for organisations. This money can be a worthwhile investment but only if the training activities provided match the organisation's objectives (Denby, 2010). Unfortunately, too often within organisations training is provided without thorough consideration of training needs and without a clear view of the objective that the training serves (Goldstein & Ford, 2002). Training needs analysis (TNA) is a process that enables full consideration of training objectives; however, it is a process that is often neglected and instead training design is often informed by what competitors are doing or what new technologies are available. A thorough TNA helps to do two things: first, to ensure that any training expenditure is properly targeted, and secondly, to provide objectives to base later training evaluation on. Mager (1962) suggests there should be three components to training objectives:

1 The desired terminal behaviour must be identified: for example, a car sales representative must demonstrate the ability to close a sale.

2 The behaviour must be further defined by describing the conditions under which the behaviour is expected: for example, the sales representative must demonstrate the ability to close a sale when working in the showroom and when all alternatives have been explored with the customer.

3 Finally, clear performance criteria must be stated: for example, the sales representative must close at least three sales each week.

Goldstein and Ford (2002) describe designing and delivering training without a full TNA as like a physician offering a patient a course of treatment before making a diagnosis.

There are a number of approaches to conducting a TNA and these vary in quality. The actual methods of conducting a training needs analysis are similar to those described in the section on job analysis in Chapter 3. Observation, questionnaires and interviews are all common methods used to collect the data that are used to complete a TNA. Goldstein and Ford (2002) recommend a six-stage model:

1 Establishing organisational commitment and support

2 Organisation analysis – examining the training climate, organisational goals, resources available, etc.

3 Requirement analysis – which jobs/roles/individuals need to be considered, best methods of TNA and process of TNA

4 Needs assessment – establishing the knowledge, skills and abilities [KSAs] of the target employees

5 Person analysis

6 Input into the design of the training and the training evaluation stage.

Gathering rich data from a thorough TNA allows for gaps to be identified and training to be targeted to address these appropriately. Bowman and Wilson (2008) outline some key challenges for TNA. First, whom is the process for? Does it represent the needs of individual employees or the organisation? Secondly, when using external trainers and consultants they need to be assured of the quality of the TNA process. Often they will be basing their training design on the data collected through TNA conducted by the organisation prior to their involvement. Finally, it is important to ensure that the data collected from TNA are used appropriately and do not disappear into a 'black hole' (p. 38).

Bowman and Wilson (2008) found that training recipients, managers and consultants saw the main purpose of TNA as focusing on business objectives. However, Palmer (2006) suggests there is a danger of focusing purely on organisational needs at the expense of the individual. Instead Palmer suggests that individual and organisational developmental goals should be matched to ensure full commitment and engagement of the individuals selected for training activities.

To summarise, organisations need fully to understand the capabilities of their workforce and the strategic direction of their business before training takes place. The training needs analysis should also provide a vital input into the design and evaluation stages of training described in the following sections. The TNA should result in clear objectives that are directly related to the training design and style of instruction that is provided to those identified to undertake a programme of training (Goldstein & Ford, 2002). The following section examines training design in detail and the many approaches and factors to consider in the next stage of a systematic programme of training.

Test your knowledge

4.1 What are the aims of training needs analysis?

4.2 What methods can be used in training needs analysis?

4.3 How should the results of a training needs analysis be used?

Answers to these questions can be found on the companion website at: **www.pearsoned.co.uk/psychologyexpress**.

Training design

The design of training is a complex matter that takes into account a variety of factors, including individual differences in the learner, the purpose of the training, the skills of the trainer and the subject matter of the training. As described in the section above, training should be based on a sound needs analysis to ensure it is effective and meets its aims. The training needs analysis should provide the training designer with an outline from which to start. This section is the largest of this chapter and begins by revising theories of human learning that can be used to inform the design of workplace training. It then goes on to consider the role of technology in training design, as there are many innovations that are changing the way in which training is delivered in the workplace today.

Theories of human learning

One of the key ways in which psychology can inform the design of workplace training is to draw from the literature base on human learning. Psychologists have long studied human learning and development, and this has resulted in a wide range of perspectives. In this section those perspectives most relevant to workplace training will be considered.

Behaviourism

Probably the best-known behaviourist study that you will remember involved Pavlov's dogs, so you might wonder how behaviourism can influence workplace training! The behaviourists were interested in the stimulus–response connection (S–R) and how this was developed and maintained. Behaviourist psychologists included Pavlov, Watson, Skinner and Thorndike, who conducted a number of animal-based laboratory experiments. What these studies have shown us is the role of reinforcement, reward and punishment in developing desirable behaviour and extinguishing undesirable behaviours.

Applying this approach to training design, the learner is viewed as a blank slate who gains new skills and knowledge through 'practice, reinforcement and performance' (Millward, 2005, p. 92).

Learning styles

There are numerous models of learning styles and these can be applied in training design. Learning styles are used extensively in education and presume that the way in which individuals approach learning varies. The best-known and most widely used of these in an occupational context is Honey and Mumford's (1992) Learning Styles Questionnaire, an 80-item self-report measure that classifies the learner as one of four types: activist, pragmatist, reflector or theorist (see suggestions for further reading for more information on these).

To apply learning styles to training design, it is suggested that the trainer simply includes a variety of learning methods in the session to ensure all learners are catered for.

Experiential learning

Kolb (1984) proposed a four-stage learning cycle: concrete experience, reflective observation, abstract conceptualisation and active experimentation. The idea behind the cycle is that the stages need to be completed in sequence for learning to take place, although the learning can start at any stage in the cycle. Some researchers have tried to map Honey and Mumford's learning styles on to each of the stages of the learning cycle, suggesting that particular styles are more suited to particular stages.

For training design this links to problem-based learning and the inquiry model. Using problem solving in training can help delegates work through the stages but it can also be time consuming and complex (Mafi, 2000). In this type of training activity the trainer plays a facilitative role rather than assuming a traditional teacher role.

Cognitive approaches

Finally, various models of human learning have emerged from the field of cognitive psychology that also impact upon training design. Gagné, Briggs, and Wager (1992) outline micro and macro learning processes. Micro learning refers to processes of attention, perception and retrieval of information, while macro learning refers to the difference between massed and spaced practice. The majority of research suggests that spaced practice is the best approach for long-term storage in the memory.

Fitts (1964) and Anderson (1983) outline a model of skill acquisition based on principles from cognitive psychology. The model can be clearly described when thinking about learning to drive a car. When we start out, we are in the cognitive stage, thinking about everything we do and often under close instruction – for example, having to think where each of the gears is and how to change gear using the clutch. After a period of practice the skill acquisition begins to happen and we move to the associative stage. In this stage, we are more aware of how the car works. We might still be making mistakes, such as stalling the car, but we understand why (we have taken our foot off the clutch too soon). Finally, after more practice we move into the autonomous stage, where we can drive the car successfully without much thought and you get that feeling of arriving somewhere but not clearly remembering all the junctions and turns on the way. This model of skill acquisition shows us how important it is to allow trainees the chance to practise what they learn to ensure that they can move through the stages and become fully competent at a task.

Training technology

In recent years, various advances in technology have been increasingly used to support training activities. You will remember from your course that simulators can be used to teach safety critical skills: for example, in pilot training. Recent developments in artificial intelligence have allowed tutoring systems to become more interactive and systems such as Second Life have provided an interesting avenue for team-based training activities.

The key question when selecting technology to use in any training programme is: does it enhance the learning? Often technology is used because it is something new, or something that competitors are doing, rather than for sound reasons based on evidence and learning objectives.

One of the key advantages of computer-based training is the interactive nature of this approach. Systems can be set up that easily allow the learners to advance at their own pace rather than being held up by other learners or forced into going too fast. Simple tests can be built in to check the learner's understanding of the materials presented. A disadvantage of computer-based training packages is the significant development cost in terms of both finance and time. This makes the approach unfeasible for one-off training sessions and more suited to large-scale, repeatable programmes for large numbers of staff.

Another form of technology regularly used for occupational training is simulation. Simulators were first used in training in the Second World War. The set-up costs for simulators can be very high, so they tend to be used in areas where the cost of getting something wrong is also very high: for example, in medical training, emergency services and airline pilot training. In these environments, the simulator often provides an ideal training solution as it enables the trainee to try out their new skills in a safe environment. Faults and problems can be programmed into a simulator and it is then down to the individual to respond appropriately.

You will know from your course that training design is a complex process that incorporates a wide range of variables, not all of which can be included in the scope of a revision guide such as this. See the suggestions for further reading for more detailed references on training design.

Once the TNA and design process have been completed, the next stage is the delivery of the training followed by an evaluation. The final section of this chapter considers training evaluation, its purpose and the way in which it can be undertaken.

Test your knowledge

4.4 What does behaviourism tell us about training in the workplace?

4.5 What are the three stages in Fitt's and Anderson's approach to skill acquisition?

4.6 What are some of the benefits of using simulators in training?

Answers to these questions can be found on the companion website at: **www.pearsoned.co.uk/psychologyexpress.**

Further reading

Topic	Key reading
Learning styles	Honey, P., and Mumford, A. (1992). *The Manual of Learning Styles* (revised ed.). Maidenhead: Peter Honey.

Training evaluation

Training evaluation can have many aims. For some, it is about demonstrating return on investment for the organisation; for others, it is about demonstrating skill development, knowledge gained, or even improvements in staff wellbeing. It could be a combination of all of these and more. You may remember from your course and textbooks that training evaluation is rarely done well, even though people know it is important (Goldstein & Ford, 2002). The training evaluation should be planned at the same time as the needs analysis and training design to enable a clear flow throughout the training programme. At this stage the criteria for evaluation should be set. Saari, Johnson, McLaughlin, and Zimmerle (1988) surveyed over 600 organisations and found that 92 per cent carried out evaluation at the reaction level. However, research into this shows no link between satisfaction and learning or between reactions and behaviour (Arthur, Tubré, Paul, & Edens, 2003). The same study showed that 42 per cent of organisations made no attempt to evaluate the investments made in MBA programmes, meaning they had no way to assess the return on their investment in these activities.

It is interesting to consider why training evaluation is done so badly. Often the reason is that those involved in training do not have the right knowledge or skills to conduct an appropriate evaluation. This is an area where occupational psychologists can really excel, using their knowledge of research methods to develop and design a rigorous evaluation process. Another reason for evaluation not being conducted well is lack of time and money. To do an evaluation well is expensive and takes time, as you want to evaluate behaviour change fully. With the fast pace of change in organisations at the moment, it can be difficult to commit the time to a longitudinal evaluation.

On the flipside it is important to consider why evaluation should be conducted. If the training has been conducted and everyone seems happy, what is the point of undergoing an evaluation? Well, without it no improvements can be made to the training course. There might be areas of it that worked well and other areas that need to be changed, and without examination of this it will not be possible to make any changes. As we have said above, training represents significant expenditure for many organisations and particularly in the current climate there is pressure to demonstrate the value of that investment. Has the training achieved what it set out to achieve? A reason must have been identified for spending money on the training activity, and without evaluation it is not possible to tell whether it achieved that aim.

The type of evaluation that is needed will vary. A lengthy, expensive and detailed evaluation may not be appropriate for a one-off training course attended by two or three employees. However, a customer service training course being delivered to a whole organisation may require a more extensive approach. One of the most enduring models of training evaluation was developed in the late 1950s by Kirkpatrick (see Table 4.1).

Kirkpatrick's model is the most influential approach but researchers today would not suggest that it is at all comprehensive. A lot of evaluation is carried out only at the reaction level, which is disappointing as research shows that there is a limited relationship between the levels (Saari, Johnson, McLaughlin, & Zimmerle, 1988).

A final consideration when thinking about training evaluation relates to methodological approaches. Within psychology we spend a lot of time talking

Table 4.1 Kirkpatrick's model of training evaluation

Level	Description
Reaction	This is normally gathered immediately after the training. It considers the trainee's response to the training and is often measured using a questionnaire.
Learning	The next level measures what the trainee has learnt from the training course. To evaluate this properly a baseline measure of what they knew beforehand is also needed.
Behaviour	The third level considers behaviour or job performance. It examines what has changed since the employee attended the training.
Results	This level relates the training to organisational performance. This is the most sophisticated level of analysis.

about research methods and methodology and this can be applied here. All of the things we talk about in research methods courses are relevant. For example:

- Pre- and post-testing – to consider whether learning has taken place.
- Control groups – to enable us to attribute any learning to the training.
- Validity – of any measures used.
- Reliability – of any measures used.
- Samples/participant selection – if a control group is used, is it matched in terms of ability?
- Experimental design – what is the best way to approach the evaluation?

So you can see how psychological knowledge can really be useful here and benefit organisations but also that evaluation is actually quite a complicated process.

To summarise, training evaluation is an important but often neglected part of the training cycle. If done well, evaluation will have been considered at the very outset of the training process alongside the training needs analysis. Training evaluation can take many forms and the exact approach will depend on the training programme being considered. Hopefully it can be seen that it is a vital part of the training process to enable cost analysis and continued improvements to be made. For more detailed information, see the further reading suggestions.

Test your knowledge

4.7 What is the purpose of training evaluation?

4.8 What are the reasons that training evaluation may be done badly or not at all?

4.9 What are the four levels in Kirkpatrick's model?

Answers to these questions can be found on the companion website at: www.pearsoned.co.uk/psychologyexpress.

Further reading

Topic	Key reading
Training evaluation	Goldstein, I.L., & Ford, J.K. (2002). *Training in Organisations* (4th ed.). Belmont, CA: Wadsworth.

Chapter summary – pulling it all together

→ Can you tick all the points from the revision checklist at the beginning of this chapter?

→ Attempt the sample question from the beginning of this chapter using the answer guidelines below.

→ Go to the companion website at **www.pearsoned.co.uk/psychologyexpress** to access more revision support online, including interactive quizzes, flashcards, You be the marker exercises as well as answer guidance for the Test your knowledge and Sample questions from this chapter.

Answer guidelines

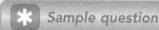 *Sample question*   **Essay**

Critically evaluate the contribution of theories of knowledge acquisition to the design and practice of training.

Approaching the question

The first thing to do is to break the question down to ensure you know what it is asking. Here it is asking you to 'critically evaluate', which suggests that you need to give your opinion as to what statements and research are accurate and indicate why you either agree or disagree with them. It is asking you to evaluate information, which suggests that you need to look at a wide range of literature. Finally, it is suggesting that you need to come to a conclusion and provide evidence for why you feel the way you do.

Important points to include

You need to think about the different theories of knowledge acquisition. What do we know about how humans acquire knowledge? What different schools of thought are there? You will need to include a range of these in your essay.

Once you have a good understanding of the theories, the question is asking you to evaluate their contribution to the design and practice of training. Here you should think about how they can help the process. Does it depend on the situation? Are certain theories more helpful than others in different situations? What evidence do you have for this? What would practice look like without the theoretical background?

Make your answer stand out

To make your answer stand out, you need to demonstrate an ability to use an evidence base and practical, business knowledge for your decisions. All applied psychologists need to show that they are able to base their recommendations on good science.

Explore the accompanying website at www.pearsoned.co.uk/psychologyexpress

→ Prepare more effectively for exams and assignments using the answer guidelines for questions from this chapter.

→ Test your knowledge using multiple choice questions and flashcards.

→ Improve your essay skills by exploring the You be the marker exercises.

Notes

Notes

5

Human–machine interaction

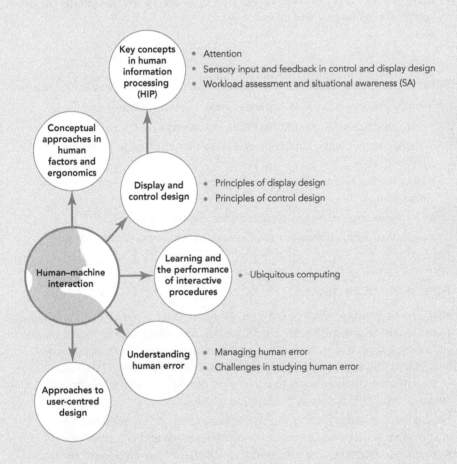

Key concepts in human information processing (HIP)
- Attention
- Sensory input and feedback in control and display design
- Workload assessment and situational awareness (SA)

Conceptual approaches in human factors and ergonomics

Display and control design
- Principles of display design
- Principles of control design

Human–machine interaction

Learning and the performance of interactive procedures
- Ubiquitous computing

Understanding human error
- Managing human error
- Challenges in studying human error

Approaches to user-centred design

A printable version of this topic map is available from
www.pearsoned.co.uk/psychologyexpress

Introduction

'Human factors' and 'ergonomics' are terms used often interchangeably, as indicated in the title of the United Kingdom's governing body: the Institute of Ergonomics and Human Factors (IEHF). The practitioner may be an ergonomist, a psychologist or in a related field (physiotherapist, occupational safety representative and so on). What is important is the application of transparent methodologies, such as task analysis and human error analysis, by which human performance data are gathered and interpreted against standards and guidance from an experimental evidence base. This is the case for human–machine interaction (HMI) and facilitates the identification of performance problems and sources of error, and the recommendation of 'usability' improvements towards the optimal human–machine interaction.

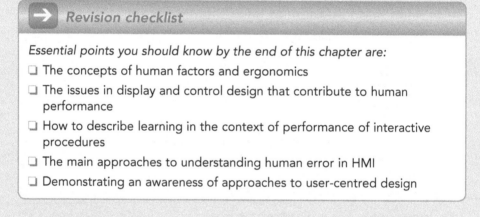

→ *Revision checklist*

Essential points you should know by the end of this chapter are:

- ❏ The concepts of human factors and ergonomics
- ❏ The issues in display and control design that contribute to human performance
- ❏ How to describe learning in the context of performance of interactive procedures
- ❏ The main approaches to understanding human error in HMI
- ❏ Demonstrating an awareness of approaches to user-centred design

Assessment advice

Assessment questions on this topic are likely to take the form of either an essay-based question or a problem-based learning task. Whichever form of assessment you complete on this topic, it is important to remember that there are many factors that influence human–machine interaction (HMI) beyond those covered in this chapter. Good answers to either type of question will draw upon issues covered in other chapters in this revision guide.

Typical *essay questions* on this topic will require you to be evidence-based in your answers, by considering theoretical, research and practical issues surrounding this topic. You will need to think about how theories of HMI can be applied at the design stage to improve the experience of the user-operator. For example, you may be asked to critically evaluate how theories of human information processing have been applied in the workplace to improve control and display efficiency and operator productivity, or how effective systems can be designed to reduce the potential for human error.

Problem-based questions in occupational psychology often take the form of a case study that requires you to apply your understanding and creativity based on the topics covered in this chapter. You will need to think critically about how to address issues including problems in HMI and principles by which to do this, in order to make recommendations for improving the utility of the human–machine interface and business productivity.

Sample question

Could you answer this question? Below is a typical problem question that could arise on this topic.

 Sample question   *Problem-based learning*

You have been asked to consider the factors that led to a breakdown in production at a Chinese automotive manufacturing plant which has recently adopted new technology and machines from the United Kingdom. This was the result of a technology transfer agreement with a major UK manufacturing company seeking to enter new markets and become a global producer of vehicles that are too expensive to build and export from the United Kingdom.

As a result of the breakdown in production, the company has temporarily suspended the local management pending review of operating procedures and staff training. An emergency team of UK plant managers and human factors professionals has been flown out to assess the situation. Early reports have indicated that a number of local employees have expressed their anger and dissatisfaction as a result of unfamiliarity with new machine technology and an increased workload. Newly appointed local managers are also concerned that their teams appear unhappy and fear that quality of outputs and wages will drop.

Outline the possible approaches you would take to understand the reasons for the breakdown in production at the Chinese automotive manufacturing plant since the new machines arrived. Provide a transparent justification for your recommendations to resolve potential issues.

Guidelines on answering this question are included at the end of this chapter, whilst guidance on tackling other exam questions can be found on the companion website at **www.pearsoned.co.uk/psychologyexpress**

Conceptual approaches in human factors and ergonomics

Differences in use of ergonomics/human factors (EHF) terminology continue to reflect the training of the practitioner as well as the overall roots of the discipline in engineering and industrial psychology. Its heritage is a domain born of the Second World War (Wickens, 1992). At this time the focus was on a contingency approach (specifying, measuring and standardising detailed components such as displays and control design) to produce performance criteria from which learning and training content could be specified for the operation of, for example, machinery, artillery or aircraft. This was about fitting the human to the task.

Today, the concern is equally with how the task is designed to fit the human and how the human psychologically constructs their task. This reflects a shift to include both a contingency and a constructivist approach to understanding how technology transforms the way work is done (Sonnentag, 2000; Symon, 2000) and includes the psychological and cultural factors that effect optimum performance in the workplace. The task then becomes an output of a broader system of interacting factors and decisions as to the allocation of functions between the machine or the human, based on optimal use of each (Jewell, 1998; Oborne, 1992). This is of great importance to the ultimate productivity and safe operation of a 'system of systems', such as a manufacturing plant or nuclear power station.

EHF professionals follow the bio-psycho-social approach (Quick et al., 1997) to understanding human behaviour. In the case of HMI this acknowledges that interfaces should be designed with these elements in mind to facilitate optimum task performance, to direct attention appropriately for system maintenance and in particular to respond to system problems (e.g. correctly interpreting warnings, signs or alarms to alert the human operator to imminent component or system failure). It is not overly inclusive to say this is of critical importance, as human error from poorly designed interfaces has been identified as a significant contributory cause of both minor and major industrial incidents, such as the Three Mile Island nuclear power plant disaster in 1977. The investigating body at that time concluded that, whilst human error was causal, fault could not be attributed to the humans involved, precisely because of the misleading and overwhelming task environment that the displays, controls and warning signs produced.

In any environment where the costs of user-centred design are constantly being debated against lost productivity, increased time to market or longer production cycles, there will be a tension between what can be done and what should be done (Harris & Harris, 2004). In an HMI context, these interactions are ably represented by the 'five Ms model' (Harris & Harris, 2004) which reflects the contemporary systems-based approach taught in EHF courses as a sociotechnical system which is simply the interactions between the physical, psychological and social aspects of the work environment and how they support or inhibit optimum performance. The five Ms are therefore: (hu)Man, Machine, Mission (task or goal), Management (supervision and established procedures) and Medium (separated into capacities of the end user as the physical medium and the individual expectations and assumptions from the cultural norms as the societal medium).

CRITICAL FOCUS

The application of EHF in practice

The very existence of EHF as a discipline acknowledges that the engineers and designers can 'get it wrong' or overlook the human involved in the safe and efficient operation of tasks such as the design and build stages of, for example, a machine or control room. They may not be involved at the design stage and so arrive later, to compensate for these oversights. Worse still, they may arrive after personal injury or some form of harm has occurred. In this context, it is not surprising that the presence of an EHF professional may provoke conflict as well as clarity.

As with so many things in life, EHF issue prevention is better than cure. A current hot topic in the discipline is to develop cost models and communicate the increasing evidence base as to the financial benefits and through-life cost savings that can accrue from EHF interventions in the process of human systems integration. In the editorial of a journal special issue on this topic, Stanton (2003) concluded that there was sufficient evidence available to present such business cases and that EHF interventions typically delivered returns on their investment in periods of less than one year, citing problems with transferable, usable methodologies as the main reason why this was not widely done. It is likely, however, that the current economic climate will demand it.

Display and control design

Both display and control design are large research and practice areas. This chapter necessarily contains an overview of the important contribution that an awareness of issues in control and display design makes within the field of EHF, such that a human-centred design (HCD) process is possible. HCD facilitates human systems integration: that is, integration such that poor design (e.g. ambiguous display notation or symbols) is avoided and total system performance is enhanced. An EHF professional may choose to specialise in, for example, cockpit design and layout for military fast jets, the design of a hydroelectric dam control room layout, or the design of the dashboard inside a standard road car. This section will provide an overview of some of the main design principles and associated challenges. Returning to the bio-psycho-social approach then, it is necessary to be aware of the boundaries within which designers of display and control systems are free to vary. These include the limitations of human cognition, which are central to human information-processing (HIP) approaches to display and control design.

Key concepts in human information processing

Attention

As impressive as the human brain is, it has limited capacities of attention, perception, memory, thinking and decision making. These abilities shift according to physiological states (e.g. arousal and wakefulness) as well as in response to environmental conditions (e.g. changes in temperature, lighting, noise or vibration or the sudden presence of novelty or hazard). The classic study by the cognitive psychologist George Miller in 1956 suggested that most humans have a working memory capacity for seven discrete units of information to be processed at any one time (±2 to cover individual differences).

A number of different theories exist for how this limited resource is meted out. For HMI purposes, malleable or multiple resource theory (Wickens, 1992) holds merit in application to EHF issues. This proposes that attention is a more dynamic resource than Miller would have suggested and that, by making judicious decisions between the use of different sensory modalities (e.g. vision, audition, smell, touch and taste), it is possible to move attention around to where it is most needed: for example, an audible rear parking sensor is processed faster and more effectively than the feedback from a rear-view mirror in the context of two or more tasks being undertaken simultaneously, as it enters awareness through a different sensory modality. This demonstrates the benefit of theory to EHF professionals. Theory makes predictions which can then be tested through controlled research design such as experiment, and can generate data to create an evidence base for safer human systems.

Sensory input and feedback in control and display design

The visual and auditory senses tend to dominate in the presentation of information for displays and warnings respectively, with the addition of kinaesthetics, the sense of movement (mechanoreception – awareness of pressure and distortion) and equilibrioception (the sense of balance, linked to proprioception, the sense of the relative position of parts of the body) to provide feedback in the signalling of alterations having been made in controls.

Workload assessment and situational awareness (SA)

In HMI terms, this can be seen as optimising human performance through balancing the demands or mental 'workload' required by the task. However, too light a workload has been found to be unsafe or error-prone in maintaining situation awareness (SA) or the dynamic nature of past, current and predictive future awareness of a task (Endsley, 2000). In conditions of under-load and/or high automation, but which still require a human to be in the 'cognitive loop' (e.g. in a supervisory role), the risks are boredom or 'labile' mental functioning from an essentially passive state.

There are a number of approaches to workload measurement and SA, characterised as physiological, behavioural, subjective and analytical. Each of these has associated advantages and disadvantages as indicated in Table 5.1. There are always trade-offs to be made in measurement scenarios and careful consideration must be given to real-time metrics, which are preferred for their validity, but incur additional safety risks: for example, a secondary peripheral

Table 5.1 Approaches to workload and situation awareness assessment

Type of measurement	Examples	Advantages and disadvantages	Context demands and HIP suitability
Physiological – secondary measures	Galvanic skin response (GSR) Electrocardiogram (ECG) Pupil dilation Blink response Heart rate (HR)	Highly sensitive and not intrusive Quantitative and therefore comparable (e.g. with resting HR) Proxy measures for workload and cognitive demands and potentially confounded by individual differences	High complexity × high HIP demand situation (e.g. busy town centre driving)
Behavioural – primary task based	Peripheral detection task (PDT) Reaction time (RT)	Low ecological validity Complexity of total task experience created by assessment process Questionable reliability Performance may be sustainable under short duration experimental high demands without a decline being observed until a 'cliff effect' occurs	Low-complexity × low HIP demand situation (e.g. motorway driving) NB High complexity × high demand situation (e.g. police fast response driver training) could be done through high-fidelity computer simulations
Subjective – primary task based Retrospective	Unidimensional or multidimensional Subjective Assessment Rating Technique (SART)	Standardised measures Quantitative SA memory probes Test/re-test reliability variable Can be rather generic and difficult to interpret unless task-specific requirements analysis	Post-primary task completion High or low complexity × HIP demands
Analytical – primary task based	SPAM (Situation Present Assessment Method) GIM (Global Implicit Measure) for situation awareness	Standardised measures Quantitative and theory-driven Formal task analysis along a time-line – useful at design stage Cannot be used in real time Variable ecological validity	High or low complexity × HIP demands

detection task (PDT) alongside the task of driving a vehicle itself increases workload and associated potential for error. A combination approach facilitating triangulation of, for example, quantitative and qualitative measures is recognised as the most robust and valid approach.

Principles of display design

Questions from an HMI perspective begin with: What should or should not be displayed? And what is the relationship between this piece of data and the primary or secondary tasks? Is it rate (e.g. mph) or state (temperature) information and does the operator need a high level of precision in understanding changes or the ability to compare easily across readings? As such, would a dial, set of dials or digital counter be a more coherent way to present this information? Once again we see that HMI is intimately situated with the task and operating conventions in that area, such that icons, symbols and notations:

- are compatible with a mental model of the task
- are universal across operator cultures (e.g. the colour red for importance or danger)
- enable discrimination in all use contexts (e.g. under varying illumination levels).

The most important information (e.g. visibility for speed and lane following in a car) should be presented close to the centre of the eye reference point (ERP) with less safety-critical information more peripherally. For this reason a wealth of EHF guidance exists to indicate the safest, most efficient dimensions for the human to operate in. These should be designed to minimise the operator not being in 'eyes-out' mode: that is to say, the visual field is the focus of attention for the primary task or ERP (e.g. hazard spotting in a car). The display field is designed to accommodate the primary task in the centre and within 30° of this ERP, so that the visual field can be scanned with eye movements alone rather than requiring head movements. Consequently, seating is required to be adjustable between the 5th percentile and 95th percentile female/male and viewing distance to display should be within 500–700 mm (Ahlstrom & Longo, 2003). The field is constantly progressing: for example, with options for head-up displays for fast jet pilots as well as auditory displays being used to augment and overlay visual displays to 'grab attention', as in the previous example of rear parking sensors.

Principles of control design

In control design, an EHF professional is required to advise on the best way to represent either discrete or continuous control tasks, referring to changing the state of a system (e.g. from on to off) or changing driving speed. In a similar way to display design, control design should be informed by HMI requirements capture that is closely situated with a task and operating conventions in that context. Knobs, toggles, buttons or other devices should:

- be compatible with a mental model of the task (e.g. in the sequence of use and location relative to their control display; feedback following movement of controls and associated responses should also reflect the sensitivity of the changes made)
- universal across operator cultures (e.g. operating logic: down for on, up for off and clockwise for increase)

- enable discrimination in all use contexts (e.g. size and spacing for those devices that must be operated wearing gloves or personal protective equipment (PPE))
- be compatible with the anthropometric movements and ranges that are possible for the operator in the operating position (e.g. switches above head height being thumb operated).

Jeremy Clarkson is a regular advocate of the Range Rover Sport and one of his many accolades involved being able to operate the 4 × 4 functionality switches and climate controls without needing to remove his thick winter gloves! Controls can be designed to assist the operator in not accidentally performing the wrong or unsafe actions, particularly in safety-critical contexts. The use of interlocks on parts-manufacturing machines prevents the action of certain mechanisms when others are in a particular state (e.g. when protective guard rails have been removed for maintenance). Other control design solutions can require complex dual-action movements to reduce the likelihood of incorrect access (e.g. the push and twist for prescription medicine bottles). This example has the unfortunate side-effect of preventing access to users with limited hand/wrist strength, such as the elderly or disabled.

The evolution of both displays and control design continues apace. Multifunctional and virtual display controls seek interactively to support users and operators through multiple fail-safes, support devices and 'nudges' (Thaler & Sunstein, 2008), creating decision-architecture aimed at maximising the efficiency with which the user operates, for example, a 'satnav' by greying out non-valid postcode digits and suggesting appropriate address lists. Increasingly, haptic (vibrational) feedback is being used: for example, vibrations could be produced by the vehicle seat as part of an intelligent cruise control (ICC) system or in a body suit for a jet pilot (Quiñones & Ehrenstein, 1997).

In conclusion, then, whilst a reductionist approach to detailing the minutiae of elements in display and control design is laudable, there is an acknowledgement that HIP and cognition are intimately linked to context (e.g. distributed cognition; Hutchins, 1995). HIP operates via concepts such as naturalistic decision making through pattern recognition and experience (Klein, 2008) in addition to the use of heuristics and biases in human judgement (Kahneman, 2011). This further muddies the waters of approaches that attempt to specify completion of 'a task'. Rather, optimal HMI is perhaps better conceived as a product or emergent property of a complex system and more dynamic methodologies are needed to illuminate this further. Traditional test and evaluation methodologies are often static and divorced from the live context. Greater use of simulations in safety-critical HMI and complex scenarios would produce more ecologically valid findings.

Learning and the performance of interactive procedures

It would not be too much of a stretch to suggest that human–computer interaction (HCI) is now required of every human in the developed world and increasingly this is stretching further by the day to the point where we do not notice we are interacting directly with a computer. This has been termed ubiquitous computing.

Ubiquitous computing: The term 'ubiquitous computing' relates to the notion that HCI has moved beyond traditional notions of input devices linked to desktops towards 'machines that fit the human environment instead of forcing humans to enter theirs' (York & Pendharkar, 2004, p. 771).

This is a contested notion, as we have all encountered scenarios that represent the 'computer says no' experience which was the central comedic line of a sketch on the BBC show *Little Britain*. Similarly, we have all encountered interminable menus for telephone banking which do not have the option we want to select and force us around several loops before accessing human help or giving up. It is not surprising, then, that at around the same time a complementary concept of the 'threshold of indignation' was being discussed in learning technology circles (Saffo, 2000). This refers to the ceiling on patience and attention that an operator will give to any system or HCI/HMI interaction which breaches an acceptable level of tolerance for them.

Notwithstanding these psychological insults, the issue of HCI remains pertinent, even in the context of moving away from traditional input devices (keyboards, cursor movement and pointing devices to access file structures and menu selection), towards icon-based, abstract conceptual models in operating systems for laptops, tablets, pads and smartphones. The latter allow for more intuitive interaction with and selection of content, but still require the learning of operating conventions such as knowledge of web browsers and using the fingers and thumb to enlarge elements or sweep them to one side temporarily.

HCI is still as much concerned with what the user cannot see, but which remains 'behind' an open window, as with what they can see. Concepts of mental models and the capacity of working memory and HIP to retain all of this information are important to consider in designing for HCI. Similar considerations apply with regard to form and function, such that a system is usable and intuitive. The more tasks a system can perform, the more utility it demonstrates. Shakel (1991) suggested four aspects to utility:

1 effectiveness of user performance (dependent on the demographic)

2 flexibility (e.g. in use of shortcuts and alternative methods to reach a goal)

3 learnability (ease of uptake and proxy indicator of interface quality)

4 attitude (subjective and affective user reaction, similar to the 'threshold of indignation' described earlier).

In considering learnability, a new paradigm in learning technology design has emerged which is related to user-centred design for determining the structure of technologies for training and learning purposes. It is called learner-centred design (Reeves, 1999). Its importance has been demonstrated in the uptake of new technology in organisational systems, and in the ultimate transfer of learning to the workplace, such that usability and utility benefits are realised in supporting and transforming how work is done (Bicknell, 2002; Bicknell, 2006; Bicknell & Francis-Smythe, 2000; Bicknell & Vaughan, 2002). In a seminal paper, Baldwin and Ford (1988) noted that any transfer of training/learning situation (such as a new HMI) is reliant upon three elements: the trainee characteristics (user competence), the content of training/learning itself and the transfer environment. Lack of attention to any one of these elements can reduce system utility and it is the job of EHF professionals to consider this broader macro-ergonomic environment alongside the micro-ergonomics of HCI in understanding HCI design.

Test your knowledge

5.1 Give some examples of when the HCI has contributed to frustration for you.

5.2 Can you explain some key principles which govern effective HCI/HMI and how these could be applied to facilitate learning and user transparency?

Answers to these questions can be found on the companion website at: www.pearsoned.co.uk/psychologyexpress.

Understanding human error

In the context of HMI, there has been much emphasis on the role played by automation in supporting and augmenting performance of the HCI operator or user. A key component of this is supporting them in error reduction by creating 'error-tolerant systems' and/or series of 'fail-safes', such as the computer recycle bin which holds deleted information at least temporarily. This chapter has debated a number of physical elements of interface design for task performance and, subsequently, psychological constructs feeding into ultimate system utility or use-value. Part of utility comes from what is not visible to the user and this includes aspects of automation, which proceed towards reducing the human-in-the-loop from a system controller to a supervisor or monitor who might have almost no direct control until the automation is turned off (e.g. auto-pilot functions in passenger aircraft or 'fly by wire' in fast jets).

Allocation of function decisions in HMI was introduced at the beginning of this chapter and automation demonstrates particular value in its potential to reduce human error. This includes the reduction of manual workload and fatigue from routine operations to facilitate increased productivity and overall system utilisation (Weiner & Curry, 1980). Think of the operations management and software integration systems that organise stock control, ordering and supply for the large supermarket warehouses, which are increasingly becoming known as 'big data'. These authors also identified disadvantages with automation, including dehumanising work, lowering job satisfaction, creating conditions for cognitive under-load and, in the context of failure of automation, reduced proficiency in operators to compensate when there is a need for manual control. These factors increase the risk of human error and so careful balance is required. Over-planning for failure of automation could double operator knowledge requirements and potential workload, increase associated costs and training, and nullify the *raison d'être* of automation itself.

We live in the presence of increasingly complex systems: for example, to manage energy supplies across the national grid. Consequently, HMI, HCI and degrees of automation are necessary to operate these systems. Some theorists argue that error is simply one of the emergent properties that will result (Senge, 1993; Stacey, 2001), that this is inevitable and that we have to decide what level of risk we are prepared to accept for the benefits provided.

The study of human error has been primarily concerned with more pragmatic issues in understanding: what can be termed an error, deriving taxonomies of error and identifying causal factors such that error prediction and management are possible. In fact, the presence of error or risk in a workplace or role does not itself constitute negligence on the part of a company or organisation (see Chapter 5), but the absence of plans and procedures to manage it does.

Key term

Human error: The term 'error' has been defined as 'An erroneous action which fails to produce the desired result' (Hollnagel, 1993, p. 29; cited in Whittingham, 2004).

Hollnagel notes that 'human error' is attributed after the event, the consequences of which are used to determine the extent or significance of the error, whereas 'erroneous action' acknowledges that an error has occurred but does not imply anything about why. This is because errors can be causal, they can be failures of planning or execution, they can be errors of recovery in a sequence of events where the intent is to rectify a problem, or they can be errors of omission, of not doing something (e.g. negligence). Additionally, Reason (1990; cited in Whittingham, 2004) draws attention to excluding random or chance effects from the definition of human error. In this sense, human error cannot have been caused by something that cannot be 'managed'. This is in sympathy with the approach of the Health and Safety Executive (HSE) and related bodies to managing human error, risk and hazards.

Managing human error

The field of human error contains multiple definitions and a diversity of approaches. Excepting notions of intentional sabotage, most major incidents are accepted to be the result of a conflated series of incremental events. This results in a 'Swiss cheese' representation of system error where a series of mistakes proceed through several layers of system 'holes' which are not picked up or not rectified until they result in the incident or disaster (Reason, 1990). What is important is to consider the implications of theories of human error in HMI, so as to look for ways to manage it. For the management of human error, there has to have been some:

● assessment of a shortfall in performance against a criterion or standard

● the potential for a human not to have acted in the way that produced the error (particularly important in attributing fault or blame).

This is a challenge for anything relying on human information-processing (HIP) abilities, which are then conflated with poor system design. As has been noted, HIP has limitations and is fallible. Indeed, some 60–90 per cent of causality, if not blame, has been put down to human errors in minor and major incidents (Reason, 1990). Even though the overall risk of major incidents is low, public concern is understandably great after major incidents such as the sinking of the *Herald of Free Enterprise*, and constructing post-event-based investigations and studies of them is undoubtedly key to uncovering improvements to reduce their likelihood in the future. Classification of human error has produced a significant dichotomy (Wickens, 1992). This is between mistakes and slips.

There exist relationships in error types and important differences in the cause and remediation strategies required to reduce the likelihood of their repetition.

● **Slips** are characterised as errors in skill-based behaviour. Perception is correct, but the wrong action is accidentally taken – hence there is a failure of *execution*. Most daily errors are slips (e.g. operating the front windscreen washer instead of the rear wiper). These are errors of *commission*.

● **Lapses** by contrast are errors of *omission*, simply forgetting to carry out an action such as an interrupted pre-flight checklist leading to safety procedures not being done. This has more serious failure potential as there is no direct feedback or recovery opportunity.

● **Mistakes** are characterised as errors in understanding. The interpretation and choice of intentions is incorrect, leading to incorrect use actions being selected (e.g. misdiagnosis). Hence this is seen as a failure of *evaluation* by operators.

   ● *Knowledge-based mistakes* result from novice behaviour as this is vulnerable to memory overload (e.g. as a result of anxiety) or the influence of judgement and decision-making biases and heuristics (Kahneman, 2011).

- *Rule-based mistakes* tend to appear in experienced users whose previous learning has taught them to be 'strong but wrong' in the presence of faulty deductive logic (if–then conditions are not completely satisfied).

Challenges in studying human error

ERF professionals can apply a range of techniques, including task classification, task analysis, error identification, fault and decision trees and/or specific predictive consequence analysis methods, such as human error prediction (HEP), in order to understand human error; or conversely, they can use human reliability analysis (HRA).

CRITICAL FOCUS

Application of human error theories in practice

The difficulty here is that the study of human errors contains a number of assumptions and challenges (Wickens, 1992):

- It is assumed that human errors are independent and can be assessed probabilistically. In fact they conflate, and slips and lapses may even occur together and mitigate the end results.

- The study of human error is largely based on the study of disasters rather than learning from 'near misses' or recovered minor incidents.

- There is a lack of large-scale or 'actuarial' data for benchmarking and industry comparisons.

- There is a difficulty in integrating machine failure data with human error data.

- There appears to be greater public and political concern to attribute blame (and achieve compensation) than to identify the cause of human error.

Notwithstanding the above challenges, systems and organisations which demonstrate high reliability and low human error rates have procedures to reduce error-promoting conditions and have been found to demonstrate the following characteristics (Reason, 1990; Rouse & Morris, 1987):

- They contain performance-shaping factors (PSF), such as error monitoring, as well as recovery procedures. They contain 'assists' such as checklists and make use of selective autonomy. They employ maintenance procedures and mandatory training in HMI (e.g. in the context of time-pressured operations).

- Work and equipment are designed to accommodate the guidelines for HMI and balanced workloads, addressing fatigue if applicable, and provide comfortable interaction with protective equipment (e.g. wearable PPE).

● They acknowledge the social interaction (sociotechnical) and other constructivist approaches to reducing human error (e.g. behaviour-based safety and management practices which facilitate 'safety leadership'; Sutherland, 2000). These augment contingency approaches by creating open communications in order to facilitate disclosure: for example, 'safety shares' at the beginning of shift and communications towards a 'safety culture' (rather relying on more negative processes like 'whistle-blowing').

Test your knowledge

5.3 How can display and control design contribute to optimal HMI?

5.4 Give some examples of how poor design has contributed to your mal-operation of something (e.g. a cooker hob with a spatially incorrect representation of dials to heated rings).

5.5 Explain the different ways in which key information can be represented to operators and when you would select particular representations or formats.

5.6 What can designers and engineers do to ensure their control and display design is fit-for-purpose?

5.7 Give some examples of how human error has impacted on you or your life.

5.8 By what methods could you go about understanding these errors?

5.9 Can you explain some of the key principles which help us to understand human error, and which would help to manage these scenarios?

Answers to these questions can be found on the companion website at: **www.pearsoned.co.uk/psychologyexpress.**

Further reading

Topic	Key reading
Display and control design (HMI)	Wickens, C., Hollands, J., Parasuraman, R., & Banbury, S. (2012). *Engineering psychology and human performance* (4th ed.). Harlow: Pearson.
New technology use in the workplace/HMI	Quiñones, M. A., & Ehrenstein, A. (1997). *Training for a rapidly changing workplace: Applications of psychological research.* Washington, DC: American Psychological Association.

Approaches to user-centred design

A weary lament from EHF professionals is that they were not involved early enough in the design cycle to address problems more efficiently. Pressman (1992; cited in Arnold & Randall, 2010) stated that a 1:10:100 ratio exists for estimating the costs associated with problem fixes at different stages in the design process. To help with this the International Standards Organisation (ISO) has produced four principles of human-centred design (HCD; ISO 9241-210). The following extract explains the intent.

> ISO 9241-210:2010 provides requirements and recommendations for human-centred design principles and activities throughout the life cycle of computer-based interactive systems. It is intended to be used by those managing design processes, and is concerned with ways in which both hardware and software components of interactive systems can enhance human–system interaction.

There are a range of different standards for different products and particular industries (e.g. defence), but all of them adhere to some basic principles as part of an iterative design process *with* rather than simply *for* users. This process is characterised by successive refinements of design solutions on the basis of evaluation data from piloted prototypes. These are measured against the initial requirements analyses (Arnold & Randall, 2010), which represent a critical dependency in the design life cycle:

● Product requirements – attributes, standards and integration issues, etc.

● System performance requirements – verifiable tasks or error rates, etc.

● Process requirements and context of use – both operational and organisational, human factors (HF) methods, reporting, nominated experts and user groups, etc.

A neat way to think about this is to ask: Who is going to be doing What, Where, for What purpose and Why? A key part of this evaluation process is therefore the active involvement of users in formative (developmental) as well as summative (final sign-off) component evaluations. Any consultant will tell you that in this latter point lies half the battle (Standish Group, 1995). Access to users (who are, after all, employees and may be geographically distributed) can be very difficult and yet they will be the first to shout when a less than optimal HMI/HCI 'solution' is delivered. All of this specification requires the application of a selection of methodologies, including interviews, observations, questionnaires, layout and link analysis, Task Analysis for Error Identification (TAFEI), fault and decision trees, checklists, Keystroke Level Models (KLMs) (see Stanton & Young, 1999) as well as experiments and perhaps even simulation and modelling for complex and costly solutions as part of the prototyping phase. It is also important to remember the need for triangulation of method and data sources to support valid and reliable evaluation findings.

CRITICAL FOCUS

Cognitive task analysis in practice

A very popular method for requirements capture in EHF contexts is cognitive task analysis (TA). This has three stages:

1 Knowledge elicitation of mental models
2 Analysis for structure and explanation
3 Knowledge representation to demonstrate the relationships between elements.

Despite its popularity, transparent audit trail and utility, TA has received criticisms. It can become too cumbersome and detailed to be usable, particularly by certain stakeholder groups (who do not have their own research staff on tap). It can come too late in the design process to be of maximum value and it does not translate or communicate well to all audiences. Inclusive design means that users must see value in it too, or you risk losing their involvement in both design and evaluation. Finally, it does not produce a design, or make judgements about allocation of function. In the consumer domain, as opposed to commercial equipment, organisations are making greater use of broader and more informal attribute analysis methods such as car build websites, so that manufacturers can make decisions about what functions should be standard and what consumers will pay for as extras. This is valuable 'customer to business' (C2B) market research and consumer insight development through networked virtual prototyping. EHF professionals might well broaden their view of methods and approaches to consider what role web-based simulations and social media could play in requirements capture, formative evaluation trials and functional decision making in the future.

Summary

The HCD process is characterised by the need to flip continually between the micro-ergonomic detail of HCI/HMI components and the macro-ergonomic issues of system performance. Inclusive design requires the active involvement of all user populations (primary and secondary users, e.g. pilots and ground crew) and this is not without its challenges. Users may not always be aware of the intended future use of a system or HMI, or the functions they currently need it to perform (its utility). Whilst there are a multitude of HMI/HCD standards and guidelines available, there is no substitute for a participatory ergonomics approach where all stakeholder knowledge is attributed with equal significance. It is suggested that EHF interventions can become mechanical and over-focus on checklists and procedures to the detriment of the experience of change and development from a human employee perspective in determining the ultimate success or failure of human-centred design.

Further reading

Topic	Key reading
Display and control design (HMI)	Quinn-Patton, M. (1997). *Utilization-focused evaluation* (3rd ed.). London: Sage.
New technology use in the workplace/HMI	Maguire, M. (2001). Methods to support human-centred design. *International Journal of Human-Computer Studies, 55,* 587–634.

Chapter summary – pulling it all together

→ Can you tick all the points from the revision checklist at the beginning of this chapter?

→ Attempt the sample question from the beginning of this chapter using the answer guidelines below.

→ Go to the companion website at www.pearsoned.co.uk/psychologyexpress to access more revision support online, including interactive quizzes, flashcards, You be the marker exercises as well as answer guidance for the Test your knowledge and Sample questions from this chapter.

Answer guidelines

 Sample question   ***Problem-based learning***

You have been asked to consider the factors that led to a breakdown in production at a Chinese automotive manufacturing plant which has recently adopted new technology and machines from the United Kingdom. This was the result of a technology transfer agreement with a major UK manufacturing company seeking to enter new markets and become a global producer of vehicles that are too expensive to build and export from the United Kingdom.

As a result of the breakdown in production, the company has temporarily suspended the local management pending review of operating procedures and staff training. An emergency team of UK plant managers and human factors professionals has been flown out to assess the situation. Early reports have indicated that a number of local employees have expressed their anger and dissatisfaction as a result of unfamiliarity with new machine technology and an increased workload. Newly appointed local managers are also concerned that their teams appear unhappy and fear that quality of outputs and wages will drop.

Outline the possible approaches you would take to understand the reasons for the breakdown in production at the Chinese automotive manufacturing plant since the new machines arrived. Provide a transparent justification for your recommendations to resolve potential issues.

Approaching the question

To answer this question, the first thing to consider is how to understand and evaluate the EHF approach and design process undertaken in preparation for the technology transfer in terms of HMI. What were the answers to the questions of: *Who is going to be doing What, Where, for What purpose and Why?* Taking a bio-psycho-social approach, what physiological, psychological and sociocultural issues might have been overlooked here?

The question states that a breakdown in production has occurred. This is serious and costly, therefore you will need to familiarise yourself with the range of theories involved in the design of interfaces such as displays, controls, feedback and warnings, and how integration of the new machinery was managed with regard to training and learning. You will also need to make some employee relations recommendations to re-engage the local management and workforce who are unhappy with the new machinery, changes to their work and the workload created by it. For example, were employees adequately informed of the technology transfer agreement? And how do they feel about this?

Important points to include

You will need to use a theoretically and practically based justification for your recommendations and approach to human-centred design. For example, if you decide to conduct focus groups with employees, who would you include in discussions and how would you communicate your findings to the organisation? Then you will need to think about your recommendations. For example, if you choose to recommend re-design of machinery, this will be costly and you will need to talk about the costs and benefits realisation and return on investment. What does the literature say about workload assessment and potential for human error, and how can you evaluate its impact on a production organisation?

Make your answer stand out

To make your answer stand out, you need to demonstrate an ability to use an evidence base and practical, business knowledge for your decisions. All applied psychologists need to show that they are able to base their recommendations on good science but also an awareness of the client they are working with.

Explore the accompanying website at www.pearsoned.co.uk/psychologyexpress

→ Prepare more effectively for exams and assignments using the answer guidelines for questions from this chapter.

→ Test your knowledge using multiple choice questions and flashcards.

→ Improve your essay skills by exploring the You be the marker exercises.

Notes

Design of work environments: health and safety

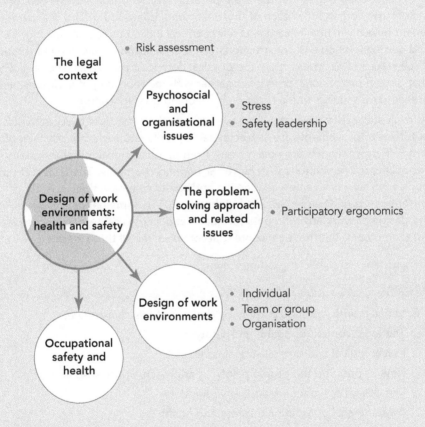

- Risk assessment

The legal context

Psychosocial and organisational issues
- Stress
- Safety leadership

Design of work environments: health and safety

The problem-solving approach and related issues
- Participatory ergonomics

Design of work environments
- Individual
- Team or group
- Organisation

Occupational safety and health

A printable version of this topic map is available from
www.pearsoned.co.uk/psychologyexpress

Introduction

From an occupational psychologist or human factors/ergonomics perspective, the design of work environments is related to health and safety through positive practices such as participation and safety culture as well as managing the reduction of hazards and risks. These could be physical risks, such as exposure to hazardous substances or other risks from the environment – electrical power line engineers for utility companies get higher pay when they are asked to work outside in the rain! Hazards and risks can also be psychosocial, such as stress related ill-health brought on or aggravated by work.

The bio-psycho-social model of understanding human function and dysfunction is clearly very relevant to guiding health and safety at work practices (Quick et al., 1997). It acknowledges that there are physical, psychological and sociocultural factors involved and that each of these elements is important. This is shown up most obviously in high-hazard and safety-critical industries such as mining, oil and gas exploration and construction, where organisations have moved through three stages of risk prevention: the physical defences; the organisational policies that govern professional practice together with the reporting of accidents; and preventative training with a focus on developing a safety culture.

At each stage they have seen improvements in their lost time injury statistics but these improvements are characterised by a plateau such that psychologists and EHF professionals are now moving from physical, through behavioural to sociocultural interventions to achieve further improvements. The HSE and similar bodies typically have safety leadership and safety culture in their 'top 10' of current needs (IOD and HSE, 2011; Johnson, 2011). Some needs and issues in the design of work environments for health and safety are perhaps more clear cut than others, but the legal context accommodates all three stages.

> → **Revision checklist**
>
> *Essential points you should know by the end of this chapter are:*
> ❏ The legal context of health and safety
> ❏ Psychological and organisational issues
> ❏ How to describe the problem-solving approach and related issues
> ❏ The design of work and work environments
> ❏ Awareness of occupational safety and health

Assessment advice

Assessment questions on this topic are likely to take the form of either an essay-based question or a problem-based learning task. Whichever form of assessment you complete on this topic, it is important to remember that there are many factors that influence the design of work environments (DWE) and health and safety (H&S) beyond those covered in this chapter. Good answers to either type of question will draw upon issues covered in other chapters in this revision guide.

Typical *essay questions* on this topic will require you to be evidence-based in your answers, by considering theoretical, research and practical issues surrounding this topic. You will need to think about how theories of DWE can be applied to improve the wellbeing of workers and improve business productivity. For example, you may be asked to critically evaluate how theories of bio-psycho-social issues have been applied in the workplace to manage job satisfaction or stress and strain, or how a defensible and robust problem-solving approach can be designed to assess and respond to an H&S issue that has been reported and in a way that is consistent with legal requirements.

Problem-based questions in occupational psychology often take the form of a case study that will require you to apply your understanding and creativity based on the topics covered in this chapter. You will need to think critically about how to address problems in DWE such as shift patterns or employees needing to use computers for long periods and what principles to use, in order to make recommendations for improving the H&S and wellbeing of workers and increasing business productivity.

Sample question

Could you answer this question? Below is a typical problem question that could arise on this topic.

 Sample question   *Problem-based learning*

As a result of your company's healthy return to work policy, you have been informed that an employee in a call centre department has been off work with 'non-specific upper limb' pain now for some five weeks and you have been asked to contact them with regard to managing their return to work. Around the same time that the employee went off sick, there were some reports about bullying in the call centre. Early reports have indicated that a number of local employees have expressed their dissatisfaction with an increased workload in the employee's absence and concerns that service quality outputs will be affected.

Outline the possible approaches you would take to investigate both the individual and the call centre context, and provide a transparent justification for your recommendations to resolve potential issues.

Guidelines on answering this question are included at the end of this chapter, whilst guidance on tackling other exam questions can be found on the companion website at **www.pearsoned.co.uk/psychologyexpress**

The legal context

Since the passage of the Health and Safety at Work Act (1974), health and safety law, regulations and guidance have required that workplaces are pre-emptively 'risk assessed' rather than waiting for a problem to present. Notwithstanding this, the start of an internal investigation and the need for a problem-solving approach would be in the context of the presence of pain or another risk factor having been disclosed in the workplace and associated with factor(s) in the work environment. This represents 'constructive knowledge' (Howard, 2000) on the part of the employer and creates a legal obligation to respond.

One major area where the bio-psycho-social model has been applied is in the study of musculo-skeletal disorders (MSDs). In 1995 almost 20 million working days were lost for MSDs (HSE, 2002) and though the average number of days per case lost was 5, the upper range included above 20 days and up to 30 days if we look at those diagnosed with stress, depression and anxiety, which typically demonstrate co-morbidity with MSDs. In terms of absenteeism and productivity, this is a big problem for employers, to say nothing of the human cost in suffering. This has led to the kinds of mass diagnosis that were observed in the 'Australian epidemic' of the 1980s where repetitive strain injury (RSI) reached the stage of being seen as a 'retrospective supplementary income'. This issue is still plagued by notions of malingering or faking, but this both denigrates the genuine suffering that is experienced, irrespective of identifiable cause or pathology, and does not credit each of the elements of the bio-psycho-social model with equal status. In legal and business terms this is unwise.

Key term

Risk assessment: 'A risk assessment is simply a careful examination of what, in your work, could cause harm to people, so that you can weigh up whether you have taken enough precautions or should do more to prevent harm' (HSE UK, The 5 Steps leaflet, 2011).

Whilst the emphasis of the Health and Safety at Work Act was on employers, the HSE also detailed legal requirements placed on employees, which include:

1 Follow the training you have received when using any work items your employer has given you.

2 Take reasonable care of your own and other people's health and safety.

3 Co-operate with your employer on health and safety.

4 Tell someone (your employer, supervisor, or health and safety representative) if you think the work or inadequate precautions are putting anyone's health and safety at serious risk.

Employers are now required to make 'reasonable adjustments' to accommodate these points and how they manifest for a diverse group of employees, including those who may uncover a vulnerability to suffering from a particular kind of physical or psychosocial stressor as a function of working in a particular environment. The legal context is also closely related to issues in the study of human error (Chapter 6), and regulations exist to cover slips, falls, manual handling, display screen equipment, noise and vibrations as well as the reporting of accidents and many more hazard and risk scenarios that may result in investigations being undertaken.

CRITICAL FOCUS

A bio-psycho-social approach to the design of work environments

In 2011/12 the UK HSE recorded that:

- 1.1 million working people were suffering from a work-related illness.
- 173 workers were killed at work.
- 111,000 other injuries to employees were reported under the Reporting of Injuries, Diseases and Dangerous Occurrences Regulations (RIDDOR).
- 212,000 injuries occurred which resulted in an absence of more than 3 days (Labour Force Survey).
- 27 million working days were lost due to work-related illness and workplace injury.
- Workplace injuries and ill health (excluding cancer) cost society an estimated £13.4 billion in 2010/11.

It is thus important on humanitarian and economic grounds to understand and reduce this cost (http://www.hse.gov.uk/statistics/index.htm)

Psychosocial and organisational issues

Both psychosocial and organisational issues relate to the concept of stressors. These are excessive demands resulting from the design of work itself. The difficulty is that these demands vary between individuals in terms of observed effects. Responses are not uniform for all.

Key term

Stress: Work-related stress can be defined as a harmful reaction that people have to undue pressures and demands placed on them at work.

But individuals experience stress differently and sufficient research has demonstrated that what is challenging for one person is stressful for another. This attribution is an important individual differentiator of stress as a positive or negative influence and it is located in a specific context. Levels of exposure and duration also have a bearing on this. The Yerkes–Dodson Law reminds us that typically, as stress begins to increase, performance improves, but that at a given point no further performance improvements are observed until such time as performance decrements follow. Psychosocial factors that have attracted research attention include: job demands and control or decision latitude (Karasek, 1979), job insecurity, role ambiguity and conflict or harassment at work.

A growing area of research is the influence of managers and leaders in creating or perhaps mitigating stress for employees (Donaldson-Feilder, Yarker, & Lewis, 2011) and creating the supporting conditions for safety leadership. In a survey of UK oil and gas workers, O'Dea and Flin (2001) found that experience of leading and managing safety environments was a necessary but not sufficient factor to effect worker attitudes to safety, and that those with a more traditional 'command and control' rather than participative style of leadership over-estimated their abilities in safety attitude development and ownership of safety behaviours.

CRITICAL FOCUS

A bio-psycho-social approach to safety leadership and the design of work environments for health and safety behaviours and outcomes

The bio-psycho-social model requires us to look at the social system of the work environment for variables that can improve health and safety. But, in the same way as leadership has suffered from a multiplicity of definitions and approaches with comparatively little in the way of comparative research, so has safety culture. There is a dearth of conceptual models specifying how these constructs are linked.

One study was conducted in Taiwan using psychometric measures of these constructs among 754 randomly sampled employees with a response rate of 62 per cent. 'Path analysis showed that safety climate (a temporally located facet of culture) partially mediated the relationship between safety leadership and safety performance. An interesting finding was that "safety controlling", one factor of safety leadership, had a main influence on CEOs and managers' safety commitment and action, and on safety organization and management, safety equipment and measures, and accident investigations in safety performance' (Tsung-Chih, Chi-Hsiang, & Chin-Chung, 2008, p. 307).

Whilst this is an example of a rigorous approach to researching these constructs, it was conducted in four universities, rather than with safety-critical organisations, and this threatens the context or ecological validity of the study.

In the case of organisational stressors, there is significant and reliable research evidence about characteristics of work and environments which tend to be associated with increased levels of stressors reported as hazards and risks, and there is potential to intervene to reduce these through job, work or organisation redesign. The job-characteristics model (Hackman & Oldham, 1980) draws attention to skill variety, task identity and task significance as well as autonomy and feedback creating a motivating potential score (MPS). We have seen the growth of participation, engagement and wellness schemes in recent years, which are intended to increase concepts of job satisfaction and significance through meaningful work as well as to find efficiencies and other benefits for the company (Jewell, 1998).

In addition to these, there are significant contributions in the EHF domain from an understanding of workload and scheduling, high pressure or deadlines, shift patterns or the threat of violence (e.g. for NHS staff) as compared to some of the hygiene factors in the environment which contribute to somewhere feeling like a 'nicer place to work' (e.g. a pleasant canteen, office space, access to daylight and fresh air, etc.).

The concept of psychological resilience has become significant in occupational areas in recent years, particularly with regard to stress responses (Quick et al., 1997). It may contribute to an employee coming under the 'eggshell skull physique' legal principle for workers experiencing either physical or mental fragility (Howard, 2000).

The problem-solving approach and related issues

The identification of hazards and risks is only the first stage in an organisational development process to improve health and safety. In order to investigate reported stressors, hazards or risks in a transparent and objective fashion, a methodology or series of methodologies are required to frame the problem, gather evidence and data, analyse and interpret the data appropriately (e.g. with respect to benchmarking information) and produce a set of recommendations on how to move forward in a constructive way that will both address the source of the problem and develop the organisation to minimise the likelihood of its repetition.

This requires organisations to:

- become aware and accept that a problem exists (observation and reporting)
- identify the problem/stressor (assessment and research)
- try to eliminate or change it (take advice and implement good practice)
- if it cannot be changed, find ways to manage or cope with it (transparently)
- monitor and review progress (periodic review, evaluation and audit).

However, the chosen research lens, to a large extent, determines what is found. Whether you are inside an organisation or operating as a consultant, you should bring (at least) three things:

- professional independence (as opposed to bias)
- methodologies to undertake research
- strategies to get things done in organisations (professional and ethical behaviour, methods to secure buy-in from key stakeholders, communication strategies, action strategies and ultimately delivery on your commitments)

As such it is important that occupational psychologists and ergonomics or human factors professionals have a range of methodologies at their disposal. In the context of health and safety, these might include: hazard analyses, cause and effect analysis (Harris, 2011), Sequentially Timed Events Analysis (STEP; Hendrick & Benner, 1987), benchmarking with other organisation or industry data, comparison of internal practices with national standards, undertaking a 'what-if' or 'pre-mortem' exercise (Kahneman, 2011), near miss promoting, inviting external expert advice, and various kinds of task-dependent risk analysis (frequency × severity).

Chapter 5 contains a critical focus on cognitive task analysis and user-centred design methods for prototyping in test and evaluation, so the discussion in this chapter will be confined to a broader evaluation process. This section is really about the process of applying scientific methods to conduct research in organisations using a 'scientist-practitioner' approach. In so doing this makes certain requirements of data in terms of the structure and controls by which it is collected as well as its scale and representativeness, so that the conclusions we come to have an acceptable evidence base, as distinct from a reliance on anecdotal evidence and 'self-generated validity'. Keeping in mind the user-centred design principles in Chapter 5, a participatory ergonomics approach is a defensible way to conduct evidence gathering followed by action phases with stakeholders firmly involved at each stage.

Key term

Participatory ergonomics: This is a procedure wherein workers at all levels within an establishment are actively and directly engaged in building or bettering ergonomic practices to enhance worker safety and wellbeing (http://psychologydictionary.org/participatory-ergonomics/#ixzz2V57ZES5f).

In beginning to construct the research we can start with the question of: *Who is doing What, Where, for What purpose and Why?* This means that the investigation must first negotiate answers to the following kinds of question:

- Who and what is to be observed?
- Where are observations to be made and how? By what measures or criteria?
- What sort of results do we need to collect? What data type?
- To undertake what kinds of analysis? Correlation, prediction, comparison, difference?
- Who is the audience for the findings and by when?
- How can 'quality' be assured in the data collection and measurement process? Consider notions of validity, reliability and triangulation (multi-source or method).

This is not an exhaustive list but it does indicate the sophistication required from the start.

The research must then balance the findings with reasonable and practicable recommendations for changes and modifications that can be made to employees' conditions (e.g. reduced working hours, refresher training) or to the work environment (e.g. new operating procedures or ergonomic supports), which reflect a sustainable position for both the employee and the company.

Test your knowledge

6.1 How can employers and employees comply with the legal context?

6.2 What model covers the approach by which ERF professionals investigate potential hazards to assess and manage risks?

6.3 Identify some examples of psychosocial and organisational stressors in your workplace.

6.4 Explain some of the key principles through which these operate.

6.5 Give some examples of validity and reliability. When are they important?

6.6 What data collection methods could you use to research a reported hazard or risk?

6.7 Explain some of the key principles which would help to manage research in organisations.

Answers to these questions can be found on the companion website at: **www.pearsoned.co.uk/psychologyexpress.**

Further reading

Topic	Key reading
Evaluation	Guba, E. G., & Lincoln, Y. S. (1989). *Fourth generation evaluation*. London: Sage.
	Quinn-Patton, M. (1997). *Utilization-focused evaluation* (3rd ed.). London: Sage.
Qualitative research quality	Seale, C. (1999). *The quality of qualitative research.* London: Sage.
Quantitative research in organisations	Saunders, M. N. K., Thornhill, A., & Lewis, P. (2010). *Research methods for business students* (5th ed.). Mahwah, NJ: Prentice Hall.
Ergonomic and human factor methodologies	Stanton, N., & Young, M. (1999). *A guide to methodology in ergonomics: Designing for human use.* London: Taylor & Francis.

Design of work and work environments

We cannot eliminate risks and hazards; we act to control and manage them. With that in mind, organisations that demonstrate low accident rates follow up the problem-solving research phase with interventions of various kinds. It is important to make these 'stick' or to embed them in the day-to-day procedures of the organisation.

The research should have suggested ways in which continual monitoring of recommendations can occur after the research and problem-solving phases have been completed. This means that key performance indicators (KPIs) need to be identified for follow-up tracking and comparisons. As well as criteria of reliability and validity of measures, health and safety KPIs need to be Specific, Measurable, Achievable, Reasonable and Time limited or 'SMART'. This allows for the demonstration of a coherent and strategic focus throughout the organisation, from the top management to the 'coal face', in reflecting safety objectives and targets, such that this focus touches everyone.

This will typically be achieved through a combination of:

- lagging indicators (lost time injury rates and sickness/absence days)
- positive safety indicators (behavioural indicators of correct personal protective equipment (PPE) use, reviews)

The second category is less reactive and supports pro-safety checks and procedures, both random and mandatory, frequency of safety audits, management and employee training and other safety activities as indicators of the continual awareness and role modelling of health and safety at work. In more recent times, this activity has progressed to include reports of health and wellness interventions (e.g. smoking cessation programmes, weight loss and fitness programmes). In this way the engagement of the employees on personally relevant safety issues is expected to mediate their relationships with safety issues at work. There is a growing evidence base that suggests this is the case (Sutherland, 2000).

Interventions in the design of work and environments occur on a number of levels and can be divided into primary, secondary and tertiary interventions in terms of their proximity to the work environment. These broadly correspond to the examples below.

Individual

- Ergonomic interventions to support physiology (e.g. disability support assessments followed by the provision of adjustable supports such as chairs or wrist rests – though the evidence for some of these is variable, not least because people do not always use their ergonomic equipment appropriately!).
- Reduced working hours or a progressive return to work following illness or injury (typically negotiated through human resources and occupational health – see the final section of this chapter).
- Job redesign to avoid exposure to particular risks.
- Work redesign to reduce time spent in static positions and encouraging people to move around.
- Providing a pleasant social environment which encourages people to interact or uses informal working spaces to increase social support.
- A range of counselling or other developmental interventions such as learning or managerial skills training to increase competencies in role.

Team or group

- Implementing 'safety shares' or 'toolbox talks' at the beginning of shifts or at specified times, where open communications are supported through 'tolerance' of occasional unsafe behaviour stories or accidents that are used as learning points. This acknowledges that humans have valid if flawed logic for behaving in unsafe ways and that this is often to do with the trade-offs between speed and safety.
- Experimenting with or implementing different ways of working: for example, through 'action learning sets' or 'quality circles' which are aimed at increasing ownership, autonomy and feedback to make work more satisfying.
- Changing shift patterns or ways of working to ones that are physiologically more sound: for example, a shift pattern that is consistent with circadian rhythms, or one that enables a more productive use of (day)time when not at work (e.g. not simply sleeping or being perpetually over-tired).

Organisation

- Auditing, for example, safety leadership behaviours and developing competency models for large-scale strategic development or layers in the organisation to promote coherent use of language, behaviours and artefacts (e.g. 'safety tokens' or other incentives).

- Auditing safety reporting and responses, integrating safety behaviours into personal development and appraisal processes.
- Implementing participation and incentive schemes as well as flexible working practices.
- Addressing bullying and harassment issues.
- Providing confidential 'whistle-blowing' hotlines and support to employees in the disclosure of unsafe acts and behaviours.
- Participation in discretionary national benchmarking processes, such as the 'Best Companies Survey', which audits related constructs and calibrates the organisation against others within and across sectors in addition to providing and reviewing mandatory safety data.
- Submitting for health and safety awards, such as the Athena Swan Women in Science Awards (supporting flexible working practices and other inclusive employee practices).
- Presenting a business case for health and safety managers and other occupational/HR professionals to sit on the board of directors.

Occupational safety and health

Occupational Health is often an organisational department where expert advice can be obtained on all aspects of the day-to-day management of health and safety at work. This can cover anything from delivering workstation assessments through to advocating or mediating between employees and managers in cases of equal opportunities or discrimination enquiries. While it works with managers and employees direct, it often works in conjunction with other departments, particularly Human Resources, and external agencies to provide, for example, physiotherapists and, in cases of personal injury or discrimination, legal representatives.

They are also involved in policy development and positive action strategies. One criticism that is occasionally levelled is that they do not have sufficient power in organisations to effect positive changes, except in reaction to a legal challenge. There is not usually, for example, a member of Occupational Health on the executive board of the organisation, unless it is a high-hazard industry, in which case this might happen through an H&S manager.

In the United Kingdom the Health and Safety Executive administers many of the guidelines, standards and templates through which the occupational health and safety service is delivered, alongside other standards relevant to the context of the organisation (e.g. Control of Substances Hazardous to Health (COSHH) standards and risk assessment templates). Whilst we can draw on information from similar bodies in other countries (e.g. OSHA in the United States), it should be remembered that the primary focus needs to remain with the specific body that represents the legal standards in any particular country and for a particular industry. And so we come full circle, back to the legal context of H&S at work and, ultimately, where the 'teeth' reside to push forward initiatives that represent 'what should be done' and not what some would tell you 'can be done' (Harris & Harris, 2004).

Summary

The design of work environments is a growing topic area as the boundaries between disciplines are blurring: for example, between ergonomists and psychologists, or between OH&S professionals and management consultants, who may all be involved in the design of new workflow patterns. Perhaps we are in the presence of systems thinking and practice in organisations at last? The motives of these professionals are overlapping and arguably they pursue the same mediating mechanisms of employee engagement and ownership, even if they begin with different intentions (e.g. some explicitly to increase the health and wellbeing of workers and their families; others to achieve efficiency KPIs, lean metrics and improvements in the bottom line). What we sometimes forget is that so long as we act within the law and set up robust benchmarking, evaluation, monitoring and other impact capture measures around the interventions we make, demonstrating changes in any of these is beneficial.

Test your knowledge

6.8 Think of a potential hazard or risk you have spotted in your workplace.

6.9 What process would you undertake to raise this? What are your legal duties as an employee?

6.10 How would you design a problem-solving process to investigate it? With whom?

6.11 How was the issue dealt with in your workplace? Was this reasonable and practical, do you think?

Answers to these questions can be found on the companion website at: www.pearsoned.co.uk/psychologyexpress.

Chapter summary – pulling it all together

→ Can you tick all the points from the revision checklist at the beginning of this chapter?

→ Attempt the sample question from the beginning of this chapter using the answer guidelines below.

→ Go to the companion website at www.pearsoned.co.uk/psychologyexpress to access more revision support online, including interactive quizzes, flashcards, You be the marker exercises as well as answer guidance for the Test your knowledge and Sample questions from this chapter.

Answer guidelines

 Sample question **Problem-based learning**

As a result of your company's healthy return to work policy, you have been informed that an employee in a call centre department has been off work with 'non-specific upper limb' pain now for some five weeks and you have been asked to contact them with regard to managing their return to work. Around the same time that the employee went off sick, there were some reports about bullying in the call centre. Early reports have indicated that a number of local employees have expressed their dissatisfaction with an increased workload in the employee's absence and concerns that service quality outputs will be affected.

Outline the possible approaches you would take to investigate both the individual and the call centre context, and provide a transparent justification for your recommendations to resolve potential issues.

Approaching the question

To answer this question, the first thing to consider is how to approach the issue as a scientist-practitioner. Taking a bio-psycho-social approach, what physiological, psychological and sociocultural issues might have been overlooked here? In terms of any hazards identified, what might be the answers to the question: *Who is doing What, Where, for What purpose and Why?* And who are the key stakeholders whom you will need to talk to for an inclusive approach to assessing and managing any risks?

The question states that an employee has been off sick for five weeks with symptoms that may well be aggravated by the work that they do. This is 'constructive knowledge' and must be taken seriously. You would need to familiarise yourself with specific literature and good practice: for example, in the design of workstations and 'healthy' office environments. What about the potential bullying issue? Where would you start with investigating this? And how might it relate to the individual case you have been given? What data might you call on and what would you look for? You will also need to make some employee relations recommendations to deal with any conflict over this and temporary workload increases as well as making other interventions at primary, secondary or tertiary levels of the organisation.

Important points to include

You will need to use a theoretically and practically based justification for your recommendations and approach to problem-solving research design. For example, if you decide to conduct interviews or a survey with employees, who would you include and how would you communicate your findings to the organisation? If you choose to recommend external expert assessments, or redesign of workstations and office spaces, this will be costly and you will need to talk about the legal requirements in doing this as well as the short-term versus long-term costs and benefits.

Make your answer stand out

To make your answer stand out, you need to demonstrate an ability to scope a problem in an evidence-based way, as well as using business knowledge to justify your decisions. All applied psychologists need to show that they are able to base their recommendations on good science but also demonstrate an awareness of the client they are working with.

Explore the accompanying website at www.pearsoned.co.uk/psychologyexpress

→ Prepare more effectively for exams and assignments using the answer guidelines for questions from this chapter.

→ Test your knowledge using multiple choice questions and flashcards.

→ Improve your essay skills by exploring the You be the marker exercises.

Notes

7
Performance appraisals and career development

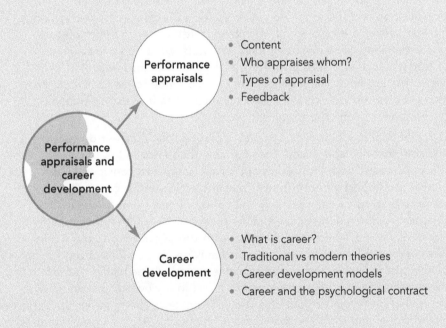

- **Performance appraisals**
  - Content
  - Who appraises whom?
  - Types of appraisal
  - Feedback

- **Performance appraisals and career development**

- **Career development**
  - What is career?
  - Traditional vs modern theories
  - Career development models
  - Career and the psychological contract

A printable version of this topic map is available from
www.pearsoned.co.uk/psychologyexpress

Introduction

The concept of 'career' has gone through many changes over the years, and the traditional 'job for life' has become less common through the late twentieth century and early twenty-first century (Woods & West, 2010). Work is now considered by many to be much more flexible (Carless & Wintle, 2007), with increased opportunity and choice for individuals (Savickas, 2002). On the other hand, where a career was perhaps once thought of as something only open to white-collar workers moving through a linear, hierarchical structure within an organisation, commonly described through the use of metaphors such as 'climbing the career ladder' (Barley, 1989), a much flatter structure has been introduced to many organisations, which in turn has reduced opportunities for progression, thus having an effect on the relationship between the organisation and its employees (Rousseau, 2004).

Performance appraisals can be a useful tool in assisting both an organisation and the employee to evaluate and review past performance against certain indicators and objectives, with a view to setting future goals that they can work towards (CIPD Staff, 2013). This reviewing of performance and setting of future goals can establish development areas that are key for the organisation to continue to perform well, but also enables the individual to have full involvement in their personal development within the organisation.

Occupational psychologists can play a pivotal role in career development and performance appraisals. They can use their knowledge of career theory to assist both individuals and organisations to consider what factors are important contributors to satisfaction and success. This can also lead to career coaching and counselling for employees (see Chapter 8). Psychologists can also help by assisting in the design of the appraisal system (which can be tailored to the organisation), the writing of development plans for individuals, and making suggestions about further development. Not only can performance appraisals be useful to both the organisation and the employee to assist in reviewing, sustaining and improving performance, but also they can enhance the relationship between an individual and their line managers (CIPD Staff, 2013). As psychologists, it is important for us to work with organisations and their employees to help them understand how they fit together and what can be done to ensure that performance is maintained and, where necessary, improved. This chapter will explore the various theories and models of career development, as well as discussing the use of performance appraisals, and how they can best be utilised.

Revision checklist

Essential points you should know by the end of this chapter are:

❏ What is a performance appraisal and why is it important in career development?

❏ How can performance appraisals be a useful tool in career development?

❏ What are the theoretical frameworks within career development and what are the problems associated with them?

❏ What are the practical and ethical issues that face business/occupational psychologists when working with employees and organisations?

Assessment advice

Assessment questions on this topic are likely to take the form of either an essay-based question or a problem-based learning task. Whichever form of assessment you complete on this topic, it is important to remember that there are many factors that influence performance appraisals and career development beyond those covered in this chapter. Good answers to either type of question will draw upon issues covered in other chapters in this revision guide.

Typical *essay questions* on this topic will require you to be evidence-based in your answers, by considering theoretical, research and practical issues surrounding this topic. You will need to think critically about the theoretical frameworks of career development and how performance appraisals can be used to support career development in occupational settings. For example, you may be asked to critically evaluate the use of performance appraisals as a career development tool, or to consider some of the practical and ethical issues that face occupational psychologists when working with employees and organisations.

Problem-based questions in occupational psychology often take the form of a case study that will require you to apply your understanding and creativity based on the topics covered in this chapter. You will need to think critically about how to address issues surrounding career development in the workplace, including ethical and practical considerations of the appraisal process.

Sample question

Could you answer this question? Below is a typical problem question that could arise on this topic.

Sample question   *Problem-based learning*

You have been approached by the HR manager of an energy consultancy firm (established two years ago) to assist it with a number of issues that the company is experiencing with its staff. The company has 90 office-based staff, including 30 call centre agents, 4 administrators, 3 in accounts, 2 in marketing, 3 in HR, 1 receptionist, 5 senior managers, 6 team leaders, 26 field-based engineers and 10 data analysts.

The managers have very strict rules where the employees are concerned, and a sophisticated system is in place to monitor each employee's time keeping, including any breaks taken throughout the day. Therefore, whenever a staff member arrives late to work or has too long a break, the management team is alerted. Any time off work also has to be booked off as annual leave, including doctor and dentist appointments, and the managers regularly keep tabs on the whereabouts of their staff, including tracking devices fitted to the field engineers' vans. There is no appraisal process in place, or any way in which staff can provide feedback to the management team.

The HR manager has informed you that the organisation is experiencing a number of problems:

1 a high turnover of call centre staff
2 a noticeably high number of staff taking odd days off sick
3 an increasing frequency of complaints from the team leaders.

You have been asked by the HR manager to implement a staff appraisal process. What issues could you face when putting into place a process for this particular organisation, and how can you overcome these?

Guidelines on answering this question are included at the end of this chapter, whilst guidance on tackling other exam questions can be found on the companion website at **www.pearsoned.co.uk/psychologyexpress**

Performance appraisals

Measuring an employee's performance can be an important tool not only for the individual, but also for other areas within occupational psychology, such as validating selection systems, evaluating training and development programmes, and succession and promotion planning (Woods & West, 2010). This section will explore the various methods by which performance can be measured and the factors that need to be considered by occupational psychologists when designing and implementing an appraisal system within an organisation.

What is performance appraisal?

Performance appraisal is the process by which an employee and their organisation (most typically their line manager within that organisation) can discuss the individual's performance and development against set objectives and competencies with a view to establishing areas for improvement and future development. Performance appraisals do not mean performance management, but rather are a tool that can be used to manage an individual's performance (CIPD Staff, 2013). They can be essential in effectively reviewing and evaluating an employee's past performance, and can not only assist the individual in their own personal development, but also improve the performance of the organisation.

Content of the appraisal

A number of factors and conditions need to be considered when designing and implementing a performance appraisal process:

- It is important to gain the support of the management team within the organisation.
- The system must be valid and meet the needs of the organisation.
- The process must be accepted by the employees.
- It must be convenient to administer.
- The process must fit the management style and organisational culture.
- The system must be supported by further training and development.

Who appraises whom?

Performance appraisals can cause anxiety and apprehension amongst those who are conducting the appraisals, as well as the employee. The frequency of appraisals can be dependent on a number of factors including the type and nature of the person's job, the structure of the organisation and the length of service of the individual. There are several ways in which a performance appraisal system can be designed, and it is important that the design is suited to the organisation, as outlined previously. It is possible for a variety of individuals and groups to be involved in a person's appraisal, including:

- line managers and supervisors rating their employees
- employees rating their line managers and supervisors
- peers rating each other
- self-appraisal
- clients and customers rating the individual
- a combination of all of the above (360 degree appraisal).

> **Key term**
>
> **360 degree appraisals**: A 360 degree appraisal is a method that uses multiple raters to assess an individual's performance. These can include their line manager, peers, themselves and clients. This method enables the individual to see how their performance is perceived from a variety of angles, and can provide more reliable feedback and an increased awareness of the relevant competencies (Randhawa, 2007). This method of appraisal does have its disadvantages, however, including rater bias and difficulty and time taken to collate data from multiple sources.

Performance appraisal design

There are several factors that an occupational psychologist should consider when designing an appraisal system: for example, how the performance of each individual will be measured and how it will be judged. A job analysis (see Chapter 3) can provide useful information about the job role competencies, which can provide attributes so that the appraiser can measure someone's performance (Woods & West, 2010). Several methods have been suggested to measure an individual's performance, which are outlined in this next section.

Rating scales

A typical measure of performance can be achieved through the use of rating scales, and a great deal of research has been conducted by psychologists to ascertain what method of rating can produce a good distribution of ratings, which can differentiate in a valid and reliable way between various employees (Fletcher, 2001). Rating scales are a popular method used by many organisations, as they tend to be easy for the appraisers to use. Rating scales can take many guises, such as verbally anchored scales with intervals that are described verbally (see Table 7.1), numerical or alphabetical scales where the intervals are not described, graphic rating scales where the extremes are specified, and comparative scales where performance is measured against other employees within the organisation (Millward, 2005).

Rating scales have been criticised, however, as they are open to many issues such as rater bias, the 'halo effect', range restriction, central tendency and contrast error. Smith and Kendall (1963) proposed an alternative method to overcome such issues as the 'halo effect' and central tendency, which takes the form of Behaviourally Anchored Rating Scales (BARS).

Table 7.1 An example of a verbally anchored scale

	Unsatisfactory	Fair	Satisfactory	Good	Outstanding
The quality of the employee's work is:					

Behaviourally Anchored Rating Scales (BARS)

Behaviourally Anchored Rating Scales (Smith & Kendall, 1963) were developed using the Critical Incident Technique (Flanagan, 1954), whereby the authors suggested that the scales should have specific behavioural 'anchors' that the employee should demonstrate, and then the appraiser (or the 'observer' in this case) should award a rating based on the frequency of that behaviour being demonstrated (Millward, 2005). This method is not without criticism, however, as Fletcher has pointed out that it can be costly and can take time to produce, and Latham, Sulsky, and MacDonald (2008) have suggested that the 'anchors' could be difficult for the rater (or observer) to identify accurately.

Results-oriented appraisal

Another popular method for measuring performance is results-oriented appraisal (Fletcher, 2008), whereby performance is measured against set goals and objectives that are to be achieved within a set period of time (for example, six months). Like the other methods, this has many advantages and disadvantages that need to be considered, as the measures are quantifiable, but measuring performance against the employee's own objectives makes it more difficult to compare them with others in the organisation.

Rater error

As noted above, there are many positive and negative aspects to the various methods of measuring performance. One important consideration for occupational psychologists is the person conducting the appraisal (the 'rater'), as there are areas for concern such as rater error and not having a full understanding of the standards against which they are measuring the employee's performance. However, one way to reduce this could be the use of self-assessments in the appraisal process (Fletcher, 2004), and providing rater training (Woods & West, 2010).

Performance appraisal feedback

We have so far looked at various types of appraisal systems and the stakeholders that can be involved in the process, but what happens during an appraisal? The Chartered Institute for Personnel and Development (CIPD) details how performance appraisals should be conducted in its factsheet. It suggests that there are five elements to a performance appraisal:

1 **Measurement** – measuring performance against set objectives, and attitudes and behaviour against organisational values.
2 **Feedback** – providing feedback to the employee about their performance, and what they need to do for future performance and development.
3 **Positive reinforcement** – emphasising good performance and only giving constructive criticism to indicate ways in which performance could be improved.

4 **Exchange of views** – dialogue between the employee and their appraiser to discuss past performance and how they can improve. Identifying any support that they may require from their managers in order to achieve future goals.

5 **Agreement** – mutual understanding of how performance can be improved and sustained.

The employee will want to have constructive dialogue with the organisation and will want the feedback to be fair, which can depend on the relationship that they have with their appraiser. The appraiser, on the other hand, may be reluctant to provide feedback (Napier & Latham, 1986), as they may see the process as time consuming, and may even lack confidence in their ability to appraise another person. Appraisals are often seen as a stressful process for all parties involved and some appraisers have been found to say nothing in preference to giving negative feedback (Smith, Harrington, & Houghton, 2000).

Feedback is important for both the individual and the organisation. The organisation may use the process for succession planning, to facilitate cultural change, and to reinforce the values and competencies within the business. The individual may want to identify their strengths and weaknesses, gain a promotion, and determine how others in the organisation perceive them. The way in which feedback is delivered is of great importance, as studies have shown that negative feedback delivered in a constructive way can lead to an improvement in performance (Millward, 2005). The way in which feedback is perceived is also influenced by the relationship between the employee and the person delivering the feedback, and how favourably or constructively the recipient interprets the feedback (Maurer, Mitchell, & Barbeite, 2002).

Whatever the design of the appraisal, as an occupational psychologist you will need to ensure that the system is not only robust, but is perceived by all who are concerned as a system that is fair and accurate, so that it can be accepted as a valuable tool for both the individual and the organisation, and upholds its ecological validity. A poorly executed appraisal system (including the feedback process) can lead to employees feeling demotivated and discouraged, consequently leading to a decrease in performance (Kluger & DeNisi, 1998).

Further reading	
Topic	Key reading
Performance appraisal	Fletcher, C. (2008). *Appraisal, feedback and development: Making performance review work* (4th ed.) London: Routledge.
Performance appraisal techniques	Roberts, G. E. (2003). Employee performance appraisal system participation: A technique that works. *Public Personnel Management*, 32(1), 89–97.
Performance appraisal measurement	Stanton, N., & Young, M. (1999). *A guide to methodology in ergonomics: Designing for human use.* London: Taylor & Francis.

Career theory

As outlined in the introduction to this chapter, the traditional 'job for life' has progressively diminished over the last few decades and the term 'career' has subsequently evolved in its meaning. The term 'career' can be interpreted in several different ways (Hall, 1976; see Figure 7.1). For example, a popular definition of career from a traditional perspective proposes that it is an advancement in a very 'linear' sense. A person progresses through promotions that externally would be viewed as a series of steps (Makin, Cooper, & Cox, 1996). Another concept is that a career can be seen as a profession, with an individual proceeding through levels of training and achieving competencies necessary to work within that profession. For some, career is seen merely as the succession of jobs that a person will have throughout their working life.

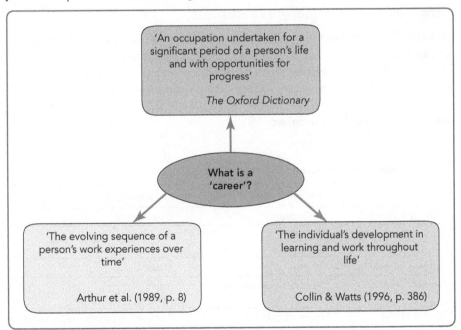

Figure 7.1 **Some interpretations of the term 'career'**

Arnold et al. (2005) have indicated that many factors have influenced the change from the traditional idea of career, including flexible and part-time working, more short-term contracts, increasing workloads, global competition, self-employment, and frequent changes in the skills required for various roles.

Further reading

Topic	Key reading
Career theory	Arnold, J., Silvester, J., Patterson, F., Robertson, I., Cooper, C., & Burnes, B. (2005). *Work psychology: Understanding human behaviour in the workplace.* Harlow: Pearson Education.

Internal career versus external career

Boerlijst, Munnichs, and Van der Heijden (1998) have suggested that there are different facets to a person's career, including the objective (external) career and subjective (internal) career. The internal career is the individual's own perception about the development of their career and the fulfilment of the goals that they have set for themselves. It is very much reliant on the person's own values and their inner feelings towards their goals, and how they measure their achievements (Baruch, 2004). The external career, in contrast, is concerned with how a person's career is evaluated by others, through such factors as one's occupational status, qualifications and income.

'Protean' and 'boundaryless' careers

Hall (1996; 2002) has suggested another alternative to the traditional concept of career, which he termed the 'Protean career'. Rather than a career being something that is determined by an organisation, an individual's career is more values-driven and self-directed, whereby the person takes charge of their career. Table 7.2 summarises the key differences between the Protean career and the traditional perspective on career.

Table 7.2 Hall's Protean career

Issue	Protean career	Traditional organisational career
Who is in charge?	Individual	Organisation
Core values	Freedom Growth	Advancement/progression
Degree of mobility	High	Lower
Success criteria	Psychological success	Salary Position in company
Key attitudes	Work satisfaction Professional commitment	Commitment to the organisation

Table 7.3 Boundaryless career competencies

Competencies	Components
Know why	Developing an understanding of your motivations and reasons for pursuing a particular career
Know how	Acquiring the professional and academic capabilities that are necessary to do the required work
Know who	Building networks, relationships and sponsors; identifying helpful people
Know what	Monitoring opportunities, threats and risks, requirements for the role
Know where	Sourcing opportunities to enter the field, develop your capabilities and progress your career
Know when	Judging the best timing for decisions and actions

Source: Adapted from *The New Academic: A Strategic Handbook*, Open University Press (Debowski, S., 2012), Open University Press. Reproduced with the kind permission of Open University Press. All rights reserved.

Another alternative is that of the 'boundaryless career' (Arthur & Rousseau, 1996), where a person's career can move across the boundaries of separate employers. The key factors to this concept are: job mobility, individual responsibility and social networks. Table 7.3 outlines the key competencies of the boundaryless career.

Further reading

Topic	Key reading
Protean careers	Hall, D. T. (1996). Protean careers of the 21st century. *Academy of Management Executive, 10*(4), 8–16.
Boundaryless careers	Arthur, M. B., & Rousseau, D. M. (1996). *The boundaryless career: A new employment principle for a new organizational era.* Oxford: Oxford University Press.

Career and the psychological contract

The psychological contract has been discussed throughout this guide, and it is an important factor to consider when discussing careers. Rousseau (2004) has identified 'relational contracts', which are typically based on commitment and loyalty, and 'transactional contracts', which imply shorter relationships between the individual and the organisation which can be more easily terminated if required (Arnold, 1996). Freese and Schalk (1996) have explored this further, and have suggested that the transactional contract is much more commonplace within organisations than it was perhaps 50 years ago, and this in turn conflicts with the traditional view that careers are attributed to a small number of organisations with long-term prospects. Rousseau (2004) examines this further, and postulates that the psychological contract can be influenced according to the career development that an individual receives.

An important consideration here is the change in organisational structure that has occurred over the years. Where once there may have been an apparent hierarchical structure in place for many organisations, a much 'flatter' structure has since evolved, whereby several layers within a company (particularly managerial layers) have been removed, thus creating a much flatter structure, and therefore fewer opportunities for an individual to 'climb the ladder', as suggested in the traditional perspective (Brousseau, Driver, Eneroth, & Larsson, 1996).

Further reading

Topic	Key reading
Psychological contract and careers	Rousseau, D. M. (2004). Psychological contracts in the workplace: Understanding the ties that motivate. *Academy of Management Executive, 18*(1), 120–127.

Gender, age and careers

Many of the traditional theories and studies on career have concerned male workers. An important consideration for occupational psychologists is the increasing number of women entering the workforce over the years, and the implications this has for the traditional perspective (Hakim, 2006). A great deal of research suggests that women are still the main care-givers in the home (Bradley et al., 2000; Crowley-Henry & Weir, 2007; Gallos, 1989; Huang & Sverke, 2007), and they are therefore more likely to have different priorities and considerations when it comes to their careers. For example, the transactional contract may be more applicable here due to work/life balance requirements (e.g. flexitime).

Another consideration is the ageing workforce. Turner and Williams (2005) postulate that there will be three million more people in work over the age of 50, and one million less under the age of 50, by the year 2022. This is again quite different from what previous research into career development has focused on. It is therefore important for occupational psychologists to take this into consideration when exploring career development.

Career development

Developmental theories

A number of theories exist to explain the development of a person's career, and two key influential psychologists in this area are Donald Super and Daniel Levinson. Donald Super (1957) based his theory on stage development, stating that there are five prominent stages – Growth (birth to age 14), Exploration (15–24),

Establishment (25–44), Maintenance (45–64) and Decline (65+). This model has been closely linked to Erikson's developmental theory (Woods & West, 2010), and provides an interesting insight into how a person may develop.

Levinson (1978) produced a similar model; however, his model suggested that there were three stages of development: early adulthood (ages 17–39), middle adulthood (40–60) and late adulthood (over 60). This particular model allows for a person to review their career to date and make changes if necessary.

The developmental theories

There has been much criticism of both Super's and Levinson's models. Super's work focused mainly on male careers, and it has been suggested that it is unlikely that all individuals will experience the succession through the stages so precisely. Savickas (2002; 2005) also argues that Super's model does not include any social factors that can contribute to a person's career development, and this view was later supported by Fouad (2007) who suggested that available resources play a part in how an individual's career may develop.

Like Super, Levinson based his findings on research undertaken with a group of male workers; however, it has been recognised that his data were incredibly rich as a result of his use of detailed and in-depth qualitative interviews (Woods & West, 2010), and subsequently Levinson repeated the study with a group of female workers (Levinson & Levinson, 1996).

What can be noted about the developmental models is that there is a common theme, whereby there is a stage in a person's life when they explore their interests and try to pursue a career that could closely match those interests. This has been supported through the work of John Holland and his theory of vocational choice (see Chapter 8).

Organisational theories

Schein

One highly renowned contributor to the field of career development is Schein (1978), who has proposed a different view of career stages and development. Schein argued that people can be classified into five main types (Managers, Technicians, Security-oriented, High Autonomy Needs and Entrepreneurs), and that people have 'career anchors' (Schein, 1982) that influence how a person's career will develop based on their values and motives. Schein's theory has been considered an important contribution as it can be a link between the career development theories and vocational interests (see Chapter 8). Schein's career anchors suggest that people are drawn to a particular career theme, which can draw individuals to certain types of work (Woods & West, 2010). Although his theory has been criticised for being focused on the managerial career, Schein does take into account the individual and the role that they play in shaping their organisational career (Millward, 2005).

Test your knowledge

7.4 What is meant by the term 'career' and how has it changed over the years?

7.5 What is meant by 'internal' and 'external' career?

7.6 Describe Hall's Protean career.

7.7 Why is it important to examine critically the view that traditional career theory is underpinned by male values and agendas?

7.8 What are the strengths and weaknesses of the developmental theories?

Answers to these questions can be found on the companion website at: www.pearsoned.co.uk/psychologyexpress.

Further reading

Topic	Key reading
Theories of career development	Kidd, J. M. (2006). *Understanding career counselling: Theory, research and practice.* London: Sage.
	Millward, L. (2005). *Understanding occupational and organizational psychology.* London: Sage.
	Woods, S. A., & West, M. A. (2010). *The psychology of work and organizations.* Andover: Cengage Learning EMEA.

Chapter summary – pulling it all together

→ Can you tick all the points from the revision checklist at the beginning of this chapter?

→ Attempt the sample question from the beginning of this chapter using the answer guidelines below.

→ Go to the companion website at www.pearsoned.co.uk/psychologyexpress to access more revision support online, including interactive quizzes, flashcards, You be the marker exercises as well as answer guidance for the Test your knowledge and Sample questions from this chapter.

Answer guidelines

 Sample question   *Problem-based learning*

You have been approached by the HR manager of an energy consultancy firm (established two years ago) to assist it with a number of issues that the company is experiencing with its staff. The company has 90 office-based staff, including 30 call centre agents, 4 administrators, 3 in accounts, 2 in marketing, 3 in HR, 1 receptionist, 5 senior managers, 6 team leaders, 26 field-based engineers and 10 data analysts.

The managers have very strict rules where the employees are concerned, and a sophisticated system is in place to monitor each employee's time keeping, including any breaks taken throughout the day. Therefore, whenever a staff member arrives late to work or has too long a break, the management team is alerted. Any time off work also has to be booked off as annual leave, including doctor and dentist appointments, and the managers regularly keep tabs on the whereabouts of their staff, including tracking devices fitted to the field engineers' vans. There is no appraisal process in place, or any way in which staff can provide feedback to the management team.

The HR manager has informed you that the organisation is experiencing a number of problems:

1 a high turnover of call centre staff
2 a noticeably high number of staff taking odd days off sick
3 an increasing frequency of complaints from the team leaders.

You have been asked by the HR manager to implement a staff appraisal process. What issues could you face when putting into place a process for this particular organisation, and how can you overcome these?

Approaching the question

The first thing to consider is the structure of the organisation and the culture that has been established for the two years that the company has been operating. Why is an appraisal process important for this organisation, and how will each of the employees respond to a process being implemented?

Important points to include

Using a theoretically and practically based argument for your decision will justify your choice of assessment system and process for this organisation. For example, if you choose to implement a 360 degree feedback process, you will need to consider who will be involved in the process, and in particular ensure that those who work in smaller teams (or even on their own – for example, the receptionist) perceive the process to be fair. Consider the research that shows that higher performers tend to evaluate their peers more strictly than lower performers, and that subordinate feedback can result in increased performance of their supervisors. What criteria are you going to use to assess whether someone is/is not performing well? How will you measure whether an employee is ready to take on additional responsibility or be given a promotion? How often should the process be run?

Make your answer stand out

To ensure that your answer stands out, you will need to demonstrate an ability to use an evidence base and practical, business knowledge for your decisions. You will need to show that you can base your recommendation on scientific theory and also demonstrate an awareness of the organisation that you are working with (in this example, the energy consultancy). For this particular question, your answer is likely to include comments about the pros and cons of performance appraisals, and how to gain 'buy-in' from all staff members, who have not had a performance appraisal system in place since they have been working there. You may also have additional training needs for any line managers who may have not been involved in conducting performance appraisals in the past.

Explore the accompanying website at www.pearsoned.co.uk/psychologyexpress
→ Prepare more effectively for exams and assignments using the answer guidelines for questions from this chapter.
→ Test your knowledge using multiple choice questions and flashcards.
→ Improve your essay skills by exploring the You be the marker exercises.

Notes

Counselling and personal development at work

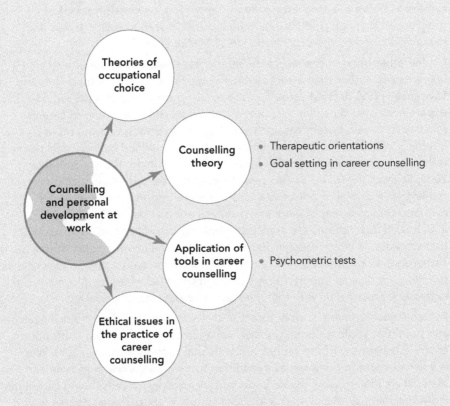

A printable version of this topic map is available from
www.pearsoned.co.uk/psychologyexpress

Introduction

Careers have been defined in a variety of different ways over time. Most often they are referred to as sequences of positions that individuals pass through during their professional or political biography; the process of successively holding various offices, duties and functions over a certain period of time (Liebig & Sansonetti, 2004). Past definitions have focused on careers as a succession of related jobs, arranged in a hierarchy of prestige, through which persons move in an ordered sequence (Wilensky, 1961). Many similar definitions refer to careers as a series of steps to be covered over a period of time (Liebig & Sansonetti, 2004), with career steps measured by the occupational prestige of positions held during an individual's professional and political life. These definitions are associated with traditional career theories that have defined careers as being oriented externally to the person, emphasising vertical progression through positions carrying increasing responsibility, status and rewards defined by the organisation (Hall & Mirvis, 1995).

On the other hand, more recent definitions have referred to careers as 'experiences' rather than a succession of jobs. For example, Arthur, Hall, and Lawrence (1989) defined careers as the evolving sequence of a person's work experiences over time, which is now a well-established definition of careers relevant to today. Recent research has described careers as being more internally oriented, flexible and mobile, with goals defined by individual workers rather than organisations (Hall & Mirvis, 1995; McDonald, Brown, & Bradley, 2005; Sullivan, 1999). It has also been highlighted that psychological success rather than material or objective success is more important to individuals' own personal meaning of work and achievement (Sargent & Domberger, 2007). Such descriptions are associated with careers described as Protean or boundaryless, in which the individual is central to their own career development and progression. However, irrespective of the career path a person may choose to follow, work is an important part of life in societies where employment is the norm, as it provides us with the opportunity to develop as people.

Personal development at work refers to the activities that develop skills, talents and potential, facilitate employability, enhance quality of life and contribute to the achievement of aspirations and personal success (Baruch, 2004). Work is a key element in our lives, as in addition to being a source of income and material wellbeing, work meets important psychosocial needs, being central to individual identity, social roles and social status. Work provides people with a sense of purpose, challenges, self-fulfilment and development, as well as the opportunity to network and build relationships (Millward, 2005).

This chapter will explore personal development at work including theories of occupational choice, application of work-related counselling, and ethical considerations of counselling at work, to show how we as psychologists can apply theory in practice to facilitate personal development in organisations.

Revision checklist

Essential points you should know by the end of this chapter are:

❑ What are the key theories of occupational choice?

❑ What is counselling theory and why is it important?

❑ What are the tools involved in the application of career counselling for personal development?

❑ What are the ethical issues in the practice of career counselling?

Assessment advice

Assessment questions on this topic are likely to take the form of either an essay-based question or a problem-based learning task. Whichever form of assessment you complete on this topic, it is important to remember that there are many factors that influence counselling and personal development at work beyond those covered in this chapter. Good answers to either type of question will draw upon issues covered in other chapters in this revision guide.

Typical *essay questions* on this topic will require you to be evidence-based in your answers, by considering theoretical, research and practical issues surrounding this topic. You will need to think about how theories of occupational choice and counselling can be applied to support personal development in the workplace. For example, you may be asked to critically discuss how theories of occupational choice can help to inform how counselling is applied in occupational psychology, or how effective psychometric tools are in supporting personal development.

Problem-based questions in occupational psychology often take the form of a case study that will require you to apply your understanding and creativity based on the topics covered in this chapter. You will need to think critically about how to address issues surrounding personal development in the workplace, including ethical considerations of career counselling, in order to make recommendations for managing potential conflicts of interest to ensure confidentiality and trust are maintained.

Sample question

Could you answer this question? Below is a typical problem question that could arise on this topic.

✱ *Sample question*   *Problem-based learning*

Alan is an Administrative Officer in the Registry Services department of a university. He has worked in the department for 3 years, progressing from an Administrative Assistant after his first year of employment. He is currently looking to progress to a role with more responsibility (i.e. a team leader or manager), but he has recently been unsuccessful after reaching the interview stages for several internal roles he has applied for within the university. Following a discussion with his line manager, Alan feels he has reached his potential in his current role but does not know what to pursue next. He is enthusiastic about personal development but has lost a lot of confidence after being turned down for several roles. He is particularly disheartened by the lack of promotional opportunities he perceives within the department, as he feels he cannot progress unless another member of staff leaves. He also suggested to the manager that he feels disappointed that he 'never made use of his undergraduate degree in business'.

Alan has been referred for career counselling by his manager. Outline an approach you would take to provide support with Alan's problem and provide clear justification for your recommendations.

Guidelines on answering this question are included at the end of this chapter, whilst guidance on tackling other exam questions can be found on the companion website at **www.pearsoned.co.uk/psychologyexpress**

Theories of occupational choice

Occupational interests are preferences that individuals have for tasks and activities that are associated with different occupations. Such interests are said to develop during childhood, most commonly as a result of educational experience (Gottfredson, 1981); however, career choice is thought to be influenced by a number of different factors including:

- careers of family members or close friends
- community/environment
- professional bodies (i.e. a specific qualification is needed)
- geographic location
- perceived work-related benefits
- chance (individuals may like the sound of a particular job, pursue it and really like it).

These factors can have varying influence depending on individual differences; therefore some individuals may seek help to facilitate their career decision making. In occupational psychology, theories of occupational choice have been well established to help individuals to clarify occupational interests and preferences based on psychological expertise.

Holland's RIASEC model

Whilst working as a career counsellor, John Holland began to notice his clients showing particular interest in or preferences for different occupations or work

Table 8.1 Holland's RIASEC types

Type	Personality	Occupations
Realistic	Conforming, practical, persistent, stable	Mechanic, labourer, surveyor, electrician, farmer
Investigative	Analytical, independent, rational, intellectual	Scientist, anthropologist, engineer, economist
Artistic	Imaginative, intuitive, expressive, idealistic	Painter, writer, musician, journalist
Social	Sociable, empathic, friendly, generous	Social worker, teacher, counsellor, nurse
Enterprising	Ambitious, energetic, assertive, self-confident	Sales person, manager, lawyer, recruitment consultant
Conventional	Methodical, conscientious, efficient, careful	Accountant, administrator, cashier, auditor

environments, which led him to believe he could develop a set of distinct occupational interests associated with personality types (Woods & West, 2010). Holland's model is based on three basic elements of career choice: the person, the occupation and the fit between the two (see Table 8.1). As such the model is traditionally arranged in a hexagon shape to demonstrate how the six types are related to one another. Specifically, the individual types are most similar to their adjacent types and least similar to their opposing type: for example, the Investigative type is similar to the Artistic type and least similar to the Enterprising type (see Figure 8.1).

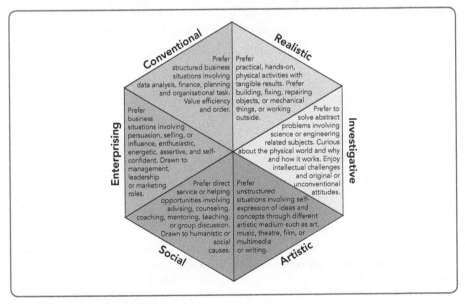

Figure 8.1 Holland's RIASEC model

However, despite the RIASEC model being well validated and one of the most widely used models of career choice, there are a number of issues to consider. For example, the majority of research surrounding the application of the RIASEC model has largely been based in the United States. As such, the influence of the RIASEC model extends to common resources used in career counselling practice in the United States, with the *Dictionary of Occupational Titles* (US Department of Labor, 1991) and some national database resources (e.g. O*NET Resource Centre, 2003) categorised according to Holland's six vocational types (Woods & West, 2010). However, this has implications for the cross-cultural properties of the model as little research has been conducted to validate the RIASEC model in wider contexts (e.g. Europe and Asia).

With regard to the measure itself, it has been argued that the model does not necessarily account for an individual's personal circumstances or characteristics associated with specific jobs: for example, if someone were to start a family or move to a new geographic location. In addition to this, there are conflicting findings regarding the relationship between the RIASEC model and job satisfaction. Arnold (2004) suggested that whilst there is empirical support for the model, in some cases the RIASEC model does not predict satisfaction and job performance consistently.

CRITICAL FOCUS

Application of Holland's RIASEC model

In order to account for the lack of focus on individual circumstances and job characteristics, Prediger (1982) proposed an extension of Holland's RIASEC model, suggesting two additional dimensions underlying the six vocational types (see Figure 8.2).

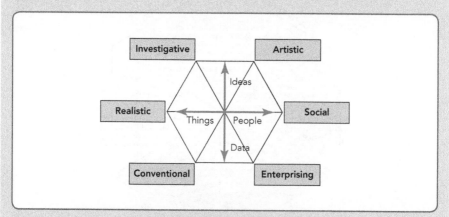

Figure 8.2 Prediger's extension of Holland's RIASEC model

1 *Things v. People* is a dimension referring to the degree to which vocations involve personal tasks (Realistic activities) versus interpersonal tasks (Social activities).

2 *Data v. Ideas* is a dimension that refers to the degree to which vocations involve creative, thinking-related tasks (Investigative and Artistic activities) versus systematic, data-related tasks (Conventional and Enterprising activities).

As such, occupational interests can be determined based on their positions on these two dimensions, which provides an understanding of preferences for tasks as well as broader occupations.

Schein's career anchors

In contrast to the RIASEC model, another well-known theory of occupational choice was developed by Edgar Schein (1993), who emphasised the importance of perceived abilities, values, attitudes and motivation. Schein described these self-perceived skills and attributes as career anchors and suggested that they are important factors in the pursuit of career preferences and aspirations. In total, eight career anchors were identified and are used in career counselling practice today:

1 Technical or functional competence

2 Managerial competence

3 Security and stability

4 Autonomy/independence

5 Entrepreneurship/creativity

6 Dedication/service

7 Pure challenge

8 Lifestyle.

In practice, clients may be presented with the career anchors and asked to rank them in order of personal importance. Furthermore, clients may be encouraged to consider the ones that most prominently represent their values/attitudes, and also the ones that do not. Similar to the RIASEC model, the career anchors are designed to lead individuals to specific occupations associated with the anchors regarded as the most appealing. However, it has been suggested that, in line with changes over time, the theory would benefit from additional anchors, such as work–life balance and employability (Baruch, 2004).

Personality, gender and careers

In general, personality characteristics are a useful tool in career counselling, as self-reported personality tools can provide individuals with increased awareness, insight and suggestions for possible future directions (Ackerman & Beier, 2003). Based upon the same principles as Holland's RIASEC model, a wide range of personality models (both trait and type indicators) are used in career counselling and personal development to facilitate career decisions and consider person–occupation fit. French, Caplan, and Harrison (1982) were the first to propose a relationship between personality, occupational characteristics and wellbeing. They suggested that the greater the extent to which an individual's skills, abilities and characteristics are associated with specific job requirements and work environments, the greater their wellbeing will be. Several well-established personality tools are widely used in career counselling, and these will be discussed in detail later in this chapter.

Gender research has shown that males and females may start out with similar career preferences, but these change over time due to experience (Hull & Nelson, 2000). However, other research suggests that males and females aspire to occupations that are associated with gender-stereotypical activities and tasks (Fouad, 2007). Many studies have focused on gender-segregated occupations to explore the reasons behind the career choices of males and females (e.g. Jome & Tokar, 1998). In terms of career success, for example, men have been shown to report a preference for objective achievements such as salary and promotions, whereas women tend to show a preference for more subjective factors, such as helping others and work–life balance (Dann, 1995). However, there is a danger in using this research to make general assumptions about all males and females, when individual differences should be a key focus. For example, research has shown disadvantages and discrimination experienced by women who choose to enter male-dominated workplaces (e.g. Dann, 1995; Demaiter & Adams, 2009), whereas males who choose to enter female-dominated occupations tend to report mixed experiences, in addition to discrimination and stereotyping, such as the glass escalator effect.

Test your knowledge

8.1 Give some examples of factors that can influence occupational choice.

8.2 What are some of the main critical issues associated with Holland's RIASEC model?

8.3 Can you explain the differences between Holland's RIASEC model and Schein's career anchors?

8.4 What does gender research contribute to our understanding of occupational choice?

Answers to these questions can be found on the companion website at: www.pearsoned.co.uk/psychologyexpress.

Further reading

Topic	Key reading
Theories of occupational choice	Ackerman, P. L., & Beier, M. E. (2003). Intelligence, personality and interests in the career choice process. *Journal of Career Assessment, 11,* 205–218.
	Baruch, Y. (2004). *Managing careers: Theory and practice.* Harlow: Prentice Hall.

Counselling theory

Career counselling has been defined as an interactional, two-way process involving a series of decisions of varying degrees related to issues in the workplace (Burwell & Chen, 2006). There is a common misconception that career counselling is designed purely for individuals who are unemployed (Neault & Pickerell, 2011). Traditionally, it has been available to individuals in the early stages of their careers (e.g. during education), but it is increasingly important for career counselling to be applied during other career stages over time (Woods & West, 2010).

How does career counselling compare to career coaching?

Career counselling is therapeutic in nature, with a focus on past experience and helping the client to resolve issues in order to move forwards. In comparison, career coaching is predominantly future focused and goal oriented towards improving particular behavioural performance (Cox, Bachkirova, & Clutterbuck, 2010). Consequently, approaches including mentoring, coaching, psychological coaching and counselling are closely related, but adopt different principles and focus (see Figure 8.3).

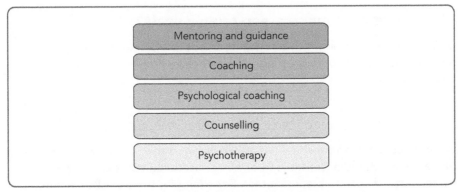

Figure 8.3 The continuum of career counselling and coaching

Table 8.2 **Approaches to counselling**

Psychodynamic	Emphasis on the unconscious/developmental stages (e.g. Freud, Jung)
Humanistic	Client-centred therapy, focused on clients' interpretation (e.g. Rogers)
• Cognitive behavioural therapy	Focus on changing maladaptive beliefs and thought processes (e.g. Beck, Ellis)
• Behavioural	Systematic desensitisation/aversion therapy – changing behaviour through conditioning (e.g. Wolpe, Emmelkamp)
• Career	Emphasis on understanding career history and resources available (knowledge, skills, abilities, interests) (e.g. Holland)

The overall aim of career counselling is to explore an individual's past and current situation and allow them to develop their next steps independently. Therefore, career counselling is focused on past experience and goal directed towards resolution of issues in comparison with other established approaches to counselling therapy (see Table 8.2).

In practice an important aspect of career counselling is the self-directed nature of the process, to ensure that the client has ownership of their own goals/solutions. In this way, the client is empowered by working towards the achievement of their own goals, rather than being instructed by the counsellor. Ultimately, therefore, this also places responsibility for the achievement of goals with the client as opposed to the counsellor.

Why are goals important in career counselling?

The purpose of goal setting in workplace counselling is twofold. In the first instance it gives the client something important to focus on and work towards. Moreover, goal setting in the workplace enables performance and progress to be measured and evidenced.

Who should determine career-related goals?

Unlike other contexts in which counselling takes place, career-related goals are mutually agreed not only by the client and counsellor, but also by the organisation itself.

To what extent are goals culturally/socially determined?

In career counselling practice, it is acknowledged that certain behaviours that are considered acceptable in one organisational context may not be considered acceptable in another. For example, there is often a fine line between what is described as an assertive management style and bullying behaviour. Popular entertainment programmes such as *Hell's Kitchen* and *The Apprentice* have sensationalised a certain style of 'management', which has been found to be effective in certain industries that are highly pressured in nature (Personnel Today, 2006); however, in some cases this can also be interpreted negatively with serious consequences for employee wellbeing.

Similar to clinical approaches to counselling, clients engaging in career counselling will often have been referred to or sought out a counsellor as a result of a problem they have encountered related to work. Such problems are commonly associated with the following:

- problems arising from the individual (e.g. flexibility with working hours)
- problems arising from the work environment (e.g. ambiguous job description/a breakdown in relationships with colleagues)
- problems arising from outside the work environment (e.g. problems with travelling to work).

More recently, career counselling has seen more clients seeking help following redundancy. Hopson and Adams (1978) describe redundancy as having a similar impact to bereavement. It is thought that individuals can go through similar phases, including initial shock, denial/acceptance, depression and coping mechanisms; therefore career counsellors may also assist under these circumstances.

As a result of this, career counsellors are required to demonstrate certain competencies to enable them to deal with problems their clients may present. Milner and Palmer (1998) describe several key competencies, including:

- active listening skills
- group facilitation skills (useful for mediating company mergers)
- being qualified to deliver psychometric tests
- a sound knowledge/evidence base to inform counselling practice
- an empathetic nature (e.g. understanding of both full-time/part-time demands, maternity/paternity leave, etc.)
- understanding of organisational and occupational issues (maintaining confidentiality, e.g. not sharing the outcome of sessions with the organisation).

Integrative model of workplace counselling

Carroll (1996) developed the first model of counselling specifically related to organisational contexts, compared with others that are largely designed for a clinical context. It was proposed that career counselling requires careful consideration of five specific stages:

1 Preparation – room bookings; confidence in counsellor; select appropriate approach

2 Assessment
  - Individual – personality, career interests, psychometric
  - Organisational – person–occupation fit/environment

3 Contracting/referral

- Explore the issue/diagnose
- If it is not your area of expertise, refer the client on to someone who can help. BPS guidelines state that practising psychologists should not be treating individuals without the correct qualifications

4 Counselling

- Goal setting, retraining?
- Link to career anchors/RIASEC
- Measure progress

5 Termination

- Number of meetings will vary between clients
- Set a clearly defined end point.

Building upon this, Taber et al. (2011) proposed that the Career Style Interview (CSI) is beneficial for individual career counselling sessions to attain a more comprehensive and meaningful insight into the individual and their progress. The CSI comprises seven introductory items exploring the client's goals for counselling, followed by items relating to six domains comprising role models, magazines/TV shows, books/movies, leisure/hobbies, sayings/quotes, school subjects and early recollections. The CSI was designed specifically to relate to the RIASEC vocational types, therefore enabling the counsellor to interpret the client's information systematically.

Test your knowledge

8.5 Can you explain the difference between career coaching and career counselling?

8.6 Can you think of some examples of the types of problem faced by individuals that may result in them seeking career counselling?

8.7 What key competencies should a career counsellor be able to demonstrate?

8.8 What are the five stages of career counselling?

Answers to these questions can be found on the companion website at: **www.pearsoned.co.uk/psychologyexpress.**

Further reading

Topic	Key reading
Counselling theory	Burwell, R., & Chen, C. P. (2006). Applying the principles and techniques of solution-focused therapy to career counselling. *Counselling Psychology Quarterly, 19*(2), 189–203.

▶

Topic	Key reading
	Coogan, P. A., & Chen, C. P. (2007). Career development and counselling for women: Connecting theories to practice. *Counselling Psychology Quarterly, 20*(2), 191–204.
	Neault, R. A., & Pickerell, D. A. (2011). Career engagement: Bridging career counselling and employee engagement. *Journal of Employment Counselling, 48*, 185–188.
Career coaching	Cox, E., Bachkirova, T., & Clutterbuck, D. (2010). *The Complete Handbook of Coaching*. London: Sage.

Application of tools in career counselling

In order to facilitate the exploration of career options, planning for the future and decision making, a variety of psychometric tools are commonly used in career counselling. As previously mentioned, personality assessment is an important aspect of career counselling as it can help to identify suitable occupations for clients. Some examples of these are highlighted in Table 8.3.

Psychometric testing in the form of ability, aptitude and skills measurement is also used in career counselling to help identify areas in which clients can demonstrate strengths and areas for potential improvement. There are a wide variety of tools available from test publishers, including measures of numerical, verbal and comprehensive ability, emotional intelligence and motivation, to name but a few. Such measures can be useful for identifying skills and competencies associated with

Table 8.3 **Examples of personality measures used in career counselling**

Instrument	What is it used for?
RIASEC types (Holland, 1996)	A personality instrument that assesses people based on six separate scales (RIASEC), of which the three with the highest scores are thought to represent an individual's type. Commonly used in career counselling or coaching settings for vocational guidance.
16PF (Cattell & Cattell, 1995)	A measure of 16 general personality factors that can be used in a number of settings, including career counselling and vocational guidance. Some versions of the measure include Holland's RIASEC types.
NEO (Costa, McCrae & Dyer, 1991)	A questionnaire measure of the big five personality factors. Similar to the 16PF, this measure can be used in a variety of settings, including vocational guidance.
Myers–Briggs Type Indicator (MBTI) (Briggs-Myers & Briggs, 1985)	The MBTI is a measure of personality that can be applied to create solutions across all areas of human interaction and personal development. Similar to the RIASEC, the MBTI is predominantly used in an occupational setting to facilitate coaching, counselling, conflict management, leadership development, team development and communication.

particular occupations to aid career decision making. More recently, Francis-Smythe et al. (2013) developed the Careers Competency Indicator (CCI) which measures seven competencies central to performance across a wide range of jobs. The CCI identifies the specific work-related skills and competencies the client has already developed, and also those they could develop further. Competencies included in the CCI are:

- job-related performance effectiveness
- goal setting and career planning
- self-knowledge
- feedback seeking and self-presentation
- career guidance and networking
- knowledge of office politics
- career-related skills.

There are also exercises that can be used to help the client move forward: for example, exercises that require clients to reflect on lists of values and select/rank order those that they feel closely represent them. Furthermore, goal setting in sessions can be facilitated by adopting the SMART (specific, measurable, achievable, realistic, time scale) template.

Ethical issues in the practice of career counselling

Adhering to ethical guidelines in any field of counselling is imperative to protect the wellbeing of the client and counsellor. In occupational psychology specifically, it is important that consultants engaging in career counselling as part of their remit adhere to the BPS ethical guidelines. In addition to this, the National Career Development Association (NCDA) (2007) has a framework of ethical guidelines to adhere to in career counselling (see Figure 8.4).

In the light of this, there are a number of issues that could arise in organisations during the counselling process. For example; if employees undergoing career counselling are working towards the achievement of organisation-related goals, it is in the interest of the organisation to achieve positive results. However, the ethical implications of this are such that whilst the organisation is expecting a timely positive

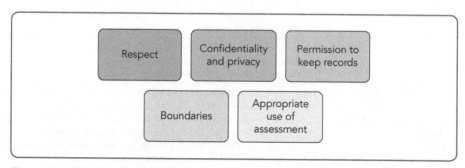

Figure 8.4 Ethical code of conduct

solution, individual employees are engaging in a private and personal process that involves building a trusting relationship, which can take considerable time. As a result, it can be detrimental to the career counselling process if there is too much pressure from the organisation to achieve results. Moreover, if progress is monitored as part of counselling sessions to document the achievement of goals or objectives, it is imperative to maintain confidentiality when discussing related information with the organisation. As such, in line with the NCDA (2007) framework, it is the responsibility of the counsellor to outline the boundaries and confidential nature of the process to the organisation as well as the client, to ensure that the organisation can be updated on the client's progress, but that private information is protected.

In addition to this, it is important to emphasise the importance of such ethical guidelines as there can be implications for confidentiality, trust and maintaining boundaries, depending on whether the counsellor is also an employee of the organisation in question, or whether they are working independently.

Test your knowledge

8.9 What are psychometric tests used for in career counselling?

8.10 How can personality measures contribute to career counselling?

8.11 Explain why ethical guidelines are important in career counselling and give some examples of ethical conduct.

8.12 Give some examples of ethical issues that could arise in the workplace.

Answers to these questions can be found on the companion website at: www.pearsoned.co.uk/psychologyexpress.

Further reading

Topic	Key reading
Application of tools in career counselling	Arnold, J. (2004). The congruence problem in John Holland's theory of vocational decisions. *Journal of Occupational and Organizational Psychology, 77*(1), 95–113.
	Francis-Smythe, J., Haase, S., Thomas, E., et al. (2013). Development and validation of the Career Competencies Indicator (CCI). *Journal of Career Assessment, 21*(2), 227–248.
	Taber, B. J., Hartung, P. J., Briddick, H., et al. (2011). Career style interview: A contextualised approach to career counselling. *Career Development Quarterly, 59*, 274–287.
Ethical issues in the practice of career counselling	Amundson, N. (2006). Challenges for career interventions in changing contexts. *International Journal for Educational and Vocational Guidance, 6*(1), 3–14.
	Stewart, J. (1999). Ethical issues in career counselling. *Guidance & Counselling, 14*(2), 18–21.

Chapter summary – pulling it all together

→ Can you tick all the points from the revision checklist at the beginning of this chapter?

→ Attempt the sample question from the beginning of this chapter using the answer guidelines below.

→ Go to the companion website at www.pearsoned.co.uk/psychologyexpress to access more revision support online, including interactive quizzes, flashcards, You be the marker exercises as well as answer guidance for the Test your knowledge and Sample questions from this chapter.

Answer guidelines

 Sample question **Problem-based learning**

Alan is an Administrative Officer in the Registry Services department of a university. He has worked in the department for 3 years, progressing from an Administrative Assistant after his first year of employment. He is currently looking to progress to a role with more responsibility (i.e. a team leader or manager), but he has recently been unsuccessful after reaching the interview stages for several internal roles he has applied for within the university. Following a discussion with his line manager, Alan feels he has reached his potential in his current role but does not know what to pursue next. He is enthusiastic about personal development but has lost a lot of confidence after being turned down for several roles. He is particularly disheartened by the lack of promotional opportunities he perceives within the department, as he feels he cannot progress unless another member of staff leaves. He also suggested to the manager that he feels disappointed that he 'never made use of his undergraduate degree in business'.

Alan has been referred for career counselling by his manager. Outline an approach you would take to provide support with Alan's problem and provide clear justification for your recommendations.

Approaching the question

To answer this question, the first thing to consider is why Alan has been referred for career counselling. The question states that Alan feels like he has reached his potential in his current role and no longer feels challenged. Specifically, he has been trying to apply for roles with additional responsibility within the organisation he works for, but has not yet been successful and feels increasingly disappointed. Therefore you will need to consider some of the factors Alan discusses to form points of reference as a basis for discussion. Think about counselling theory and what approach might be appropriate to take forward with Alan. Where does Alan's problem appear to arise from?

Important points to include

You will need to use a theoretically and practically based justification for your approach to career counselling with Alan. For example, what are the stages of counselling and why are they important to plan for? Would you include psychometrics in your discussions with Alan and how would you use this information? Furthermore, how would you communicate your findings to the organisation/Alan's manager? What are the ethical implications of sharing information with others and how would you adhere to ethical standards?

Make your answer stand out

To make your answer stand out, you need to demonstrate an ability to use an evidence base and practical, business knowledge for your decisions. All applied psychologists need to show that they are able to base their recommendations on good science but also to demonstrate an awareness of the client they are working with. In this answer it would be beneficial to comment on the implications of working with a client as an independent consultant, as opposed to working in a career counselling service employed by the same organisation. Also, think about potential implications of Alan being referred to counselling by his manager. Therefore, recommendations could also include the exploration of Alan's attitude towards counselling. Has he ever had counselling before? Information of this nature can impact upon the counselling process.

Explore the accompanying website at www.pearsoned.co.uk/psychologyexpress
→ Prepare more effectively for exams and assignments using the answer guidelines for questions from this chapter.
→ Test your knowledge using multiple choice questions and flashcards.
→ Improve your essay skills by exploring the You be the marker exercises.

Notes

9

Employee relations and motivation

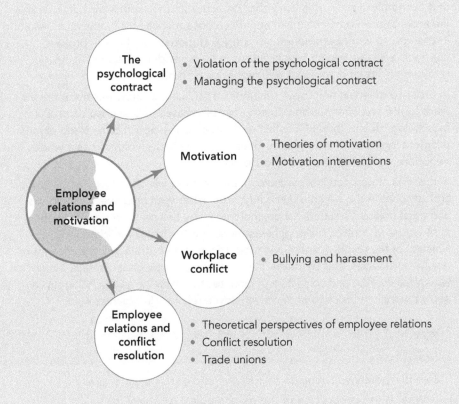

- **The psychological contract**
  - Violation of the psychological contract
  - Managing the psychological contract

- **Employee relations and motivation**

- **Motivation**
  - Theories of motivation
  - Motivation interventions

- **Workplace conflict**
  - Bullying and harassment

- **Employee relations and conflict resolution**
  - Theoretical perspectives of employee relations
  - Conflict resolution
  - Trade unions

A printable version of this topic map is available from
www.pearsoned.co.uk/psychologyexpress

Introduction

Employee relations, also known as industrial relations, refers to the maintenance of the relationship between employer and employee. This relationship is of paramount importance as it contributes to productivity, motivation and morale in the workplace (Millward, 2005). The workplace environment is also influenced by contextual factors that shape the outcomes of these relationships, such as employment terms, contracts and conflict (Pyman et al., 2010).

Individuals will often have a set of expectations and beliefs about the employment relationship, in addition to the written contracts and documents that are issued at the beginning of employment. These expectations and beliefs are known as the psychological contract. As a result of the individual nature of the psychological contract and the ever changing business environment and economic climate, it is likely that breaches and violations will occur. In this instance, broken contracts have negative consequences for employees, resulting in changes to work behaviours, attitudes and motivation. In turn, broken contracts will also impact organisations in terms of decreased productivity, reduced loyalty of employees and higher staff turnover.

In order to maintain employee relations, organisations known as trade unions were formed to offer support to employees in cases of breached contracts (psychological and formal), conflict and other issues. Specifically, trade unions promote legislation favourable to their members and employees as a whole, and negotiate with employers on their behalf.

In this area of occupational psychology, practitioners will often focus on behaviour and attitudes in the workplace and interactions between employees, employers and trade unions. Occupational psychologists may be called upon to intervene in situations of conflict, bullying, harassment or other issues associated with a violation of the employment relationship, to implement strategies that prevent or resolve such issues. This chapter will explore the psychological contract, motivation, workplace conflict, and conflict resolution, to show how we as psychologists can apply theory in practice to promote employee relations in organisations.

→ Revision checklist

Essential points you should know by the end of this chapter are:
❏ What is the importance of the psychological contract?
❏ What are the key approaches to motivation and how can they be used to enhance motivation and productivity in organisations?
❏ How can workplace conflict arise, including bullying and harassment?
❏ What is conflict resolution and maintaining employee relations?
❏ What is the role of trade unions in employee relations?

Assessment advice

Assessment questions on this topic are likely to take the form of either an essay-based question or a problem-based learning task. Whichever form of assessment you complete on this topic, it is important to remember that there are many factors that influence employee relations beyond those covered in this chapter. Good answers to either type of question will draw upon issues covered in other chapters in this revision guide.

Typical *essay questions* on this topic will require you to be evidence-based in your answers, by considering theoretical, research and practical issues surrounding this topic. You will need to think about how theories of motivation, workplace conflict and conflict resolution can be applied to maintain employee relations in occupational settings. For example, you may be asked to critically evaluate how theories of motivation have been used in the workplace to encourage employee productivity, or how effective trade unions are in managing workplace conflict.

Problem-based questions in occupational psychology often take the form of a case study that will require you to apply your understanding and creativity based on the topics covered in this chapter. You will need to think critically about how to address issues including breaches or violations of the psychological contract and poor employee relations in the workplace, in order to make recommendations for improving employee motivation and resolution of workplace conflict.

Sample question

Could you answer this question? Below is a typical problem question that could arise on this topic.

 Sample question   *Problem-based learning*

You have been asked to consider the factors that led to a breakdown in employee relations in two UK customer service centres that have recently merged. As a result of the merger, the company has closed a major call centre (resulting in several redundancies) and undergone a management restructure.

Several employees who are now based in the new call centre have expressed their anger and dissatisfaction as a result of unfamiliarity with new company procedures and an increased workload. Newly appointed managers are also concerned that their teams appear unhappy and fear that quality of customer service will be affected.

Outline the possible approaches you would take to maintain employee relations at the customer service centre, and provide a clear justification for your recommendations.

Guidelines on answering this question are included at the end of this chapter, whilst guidance on tackling other exam questions can be found on the companion website at **www.pearsoned.co.uk/psychologyexpress**

The psychological contract

The psychological contract represents the mutual beliefs, expectations and informal obligations between employer and employee (Jafri, 2011). It is quite different from a formal written contract of employment as that usually contains the actual duties and responsibilities associated with a job. In this respect the psychological contract is highly dynamic in nature as perceptions and expectations will vary from person to person. As a result of this, breaches or violations of the psychological contract are quite common. For example, there could be a team of employees all doing the same job, but their beliefs and expectations may differ completely.

Violation of the psychological contract

The psychological contract can be violated in a number of different ways and by a number of different people (see Table 9.1). For example, recruiters, managers, co-workers, mentors and managers can contribute to contract violations as a result of giving mixed messages, few interactions, lack of support, making promises with little follow-through, and unfamiliarity with the job.

The consequences of a broken psychological contract can be particularly negative for the employee and the organisation. From an employee's perspective a considerable amount of time is spent at work, therefore it is often thought that the same negative emotions can be experienced in response to a contract

Table 9.1 Types of psychological contract violation

Type of violation	Explanation	Example
Inadvertent violation	Your expectations may differ from other people's, therefore behaviours and actions are interpreted differently.	One person in a team appears not to be doing their job.
Disruption	It may be difficult or impossible to fulfil your expectations, despite a willingness to do so.	You may not receive an annual bonus, as a result of the current economic climate.
Breach of contract	You or your employer refuse to fulfil the contract (e.g. the written employment contract).	You refuse to do overtime.

violation as are associated with conflicts experienced at home. Consequences of contract violations can include:

- initial outrage, shock, resentment, anger
- reduced trust
- decreased job satisfaction
- low productivity
- poor attendance
- decreased commitment.

All of these can result in increased staff turnover for the organisation.

Employees have been known to respond to violations of the psychological contract in a number of different ways that can be damaging to organisations (Nadin & Williams, 2012) (see Figure 9.1).

Employee 'voice' is very important in response to a contract violation. It is a powerful way for employees to make their feelings known to an organisation. Employees will often use their 'voice' to try and influence the other party involved in the contract breach and this can be done in either a constructive or destructive way. For example, some organisations may adopt a very open approach with their employees, enabling their employees to voice their feedback and opinions. In particular, anonymous feedback systems are thought to be most effective as they encourage employees to voice their opinions without fear of the consequences. In this way, employees will be able to see that issues are being acknowledged and dealt with, and a positive relationship can often be restored. In contrast to this, employees can respond to violations in a more destructive way, often resulting in their exit from the organisation. Exit from an organisation will occur when attempts to fix the problem have failed. In the meantime, employees may either actively seek to cause damage or sabotage the organisation, or adopt a passive approach, often continuing their job but in a half-hearted or non-caring manner.

Managing the psychological contract

In order to manage the psychological contract effectively, efforts can be made by both employers and employees to maintain a positive and trusting relationship

	Constructive	Destructive
Active	Voice	Exit/destruction
Passive	Loyalty/silence	Neglect/silence

Figure 9.1 Employees' responses to psychological contract violations

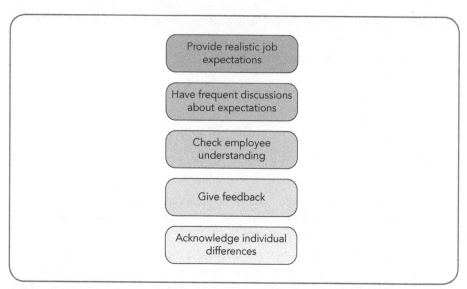

Figure 9.2 Steps to enable employers and employees to manage the psychological contract

(see Figure 9.2). In particular, it is important for employers to acknowledge individual differences amongst their employees, as different people are motivated by different things.

Violations of the psychological contract can be avoided by employees and employers if the following questions are considered by both parties:

1 How can you ensure the psychological contract is not broken?

2 What do employees/employers do that you would consider a breach of the contract?

3 What is most important to you to have in the psychological contract?

4 How would you ensure the psychological contract with the employee/ employer remains?

Further reading

Topic	Key reading
The psychological contract	Conway, N., & Briner, R. B. (2005). *Understanding psychological contracts at work: A critical evaluation of theory and research.* Maidenhead: Open University Press.

Motivation

There are many definitions of motivation, which all literally refer to the desire individuals have to do things. In terms of work, Pinder (2008) describes motivation as the internal and external forces that initiate work-related action and it is a crucial element in goal setting and achievement. Motivation is manifested by attention, effort and persistence (Tremblay et al., 2009). The ability to measure factors that energise, channel and sustain work behaviour over time (Steers, Mowday, & Shapiro, 2004) is essential for capturing employee motivation and for developing interventions aimed at enhancing motivation and, in turn, job satisfaction and performance. In essence, skills and abilities tests or training will help to determine whether individuals *can* do something, whereas motivation determines whether individuals *will* do something.

Theories of motivation

Theories of motivation were traditionally based around basic human needs. Since then theories have been developed that focus more on cognition and disposition, with emphasis on how choices are made and goal setting (Millward, 2005).

Needs-based theories

In 1954, Abraham Maslow developed a theory of human motivation known as the *hierarchy of needs*. It is often portrayed in the shape of a pyramid, with the most basic needs at the bottom and the need for 'self-actualisation', or reaching one's full potential, at the top (see Figure 9.3).

Once needs are satisfied at each level of the pyramid, individuals work their way up the hierarchy. This theory is well known in psychology as a whole and in the field of motivation; therefore it is important for occupational psychologists to see how it can apply to the workplace. For example, organisations demonstrate they are committed to helping employees identify, pursue and achieve their unique personal potential so that when individuals reach self-actualisation, they become more valuable as employees.

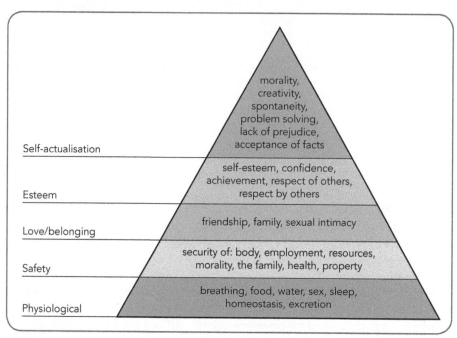

Figure 9.3 Maslow's hierarchy of needs

Similarly, the *two-factor theory* (Herzberg, Mausner, & Snyderman, 1959) suggests that individuals have two basic needs to maintain motivation:

- *hygiene needs* (e.g. work conditions, salary, relationship with colleagues, security)
- *motivators* (e.g. feedback, praise, responsibility, advancement).

This theory was one of the first to link motivation to work, suggesting that individuals have basic needs to prevent de-motivation, enabling them to do their job. In particular, this theory emphasises how the factors that motivate people at work are different from the factors that cause job dissatisfaction, and not simply the opposite of the factors that cause dissatisfaction. For example, if it is assumed that employees are only motivated by addressing hygiene needs, it is likely that employees will experience job dissatisfaction. In contrast, organisations that provide the environment for employees to pursue and satisfy the factors that are motivational (i.e. achievement, development, feedback), in addition to hygiene needs, will enable employees to achieve satisfaction at work.

CRITICAL FOCUS

Application of needs-based theories in practice

In practice, needs-based theories of motivation suggest that basic needs and values come from the individual and cannot be established by management practices or organisational factors. Assumptions of these theories suggest that needs are innate

▶

and can never change, therefore fulfilment of needs can be described as a closed system, in that if needs are unfulfilled then individuals experience a state of imbalance. As a result of this, efforts by managers and organisations can facilitate goal setting to achieve unfulfilled needs, but are not considered a source of motivation. According to needs-based theories, needs are either met or not, which often ignores cognition and behaviour.

Process-based theory

Expectancy theory (Vroom, 1964) was the first to suggest that employee performance and motivation is based on individual factors such as personality, skills, abilities, knowledge and experience. The theory can be applied in the workplace by identifying three key elements that lead to motivation: expectancy (i.e. effort), instrumentality (i.e. performance) and valence (i.e. outcome).

This theory describes motivation as a conscious process, relating employees' values, competencies, personality traits and environmental support (colleague support, quality of equipment/materials, availability of information and experience of previous success at tasks) to motivation. In consultancy this theory has many applications – for example, if an organisation provides the opportunity for employees to register for an external, residential work-related training course, employees may consider the following:

● Expectancy – do I want to pursue my personal development?

● Instrumentality – is taking the time to work away from home worth it?

● Valence – will the outcome of the training opportunity benefit me?

In essence, employees' motivation to behave in a certain way (i.e. pursue personal development at a residential training course) is determined by the desirability of the outcome (i.e. the value of the new skills and experience acquired from the training programme). Expectancy theory of motivation recognises the role of independent thought in decision making and goal-directed behaviour. However, many researchers have suggested that the cognitive processes involved in such decision making are too complex and not necessary when individuals are presented with a choice where alternatives are clear and information is readily available (Beach & Connolly, 2005; Lord, Hanges, & Godfrey, 2003; Tharanou, 2001).

Equity theory

Equity theory of motivation was developed by Adams (1963) and has its roots in behaviourism. It suggests that motivation is related to equity, in that employees seek to maintain fairness between the inputs they bring to their job and the outputs they receive from it. In particular, equity theory suggests employees are motivated to maintain their perceived fairness at work by comparing themselves to others (i.e. colleagues in similar positions/situations to themselves). In contrast to other theories of motivation, equity theory offers an explanation for why basic needs and working conditions alone do not determine motivation (see Figure 9.4).

If employees perceive an imbalance between their own efforts and those of others, it is likely that they will become demotivated. Equity theory therefore has implications for employee morale, productivity and staff turnover in organisations, as it is suggested that employees will respond to perceptions of inequity in a number of ways, for example:

- develop an incorrect perception of inputs/outputs
- directly alter inputs (e.g. decreased effort, determination, commitment)
- exit the organisation.

Goal-setting theory

Goal setting and appropriate feedback are linked to task performance and motivation (Latham & Pinder, 2005). Originally, Locke and Latham (1976) developed a goal-setting theory of motivation, which emphasised the idea that goal setting encourages employees to focus on a manageable process with achievable outcomes. The principles of goal-setting theory can be applied to the workplace as follows:

- Employees' *willingness* to work towards the achievement of goals is a key source of motivation.
- Employee commitment to goals, especially when goals are challenging rather than simplistic or vague and when employees have been involved in the goal-setting process, is key to maintaining motivation.

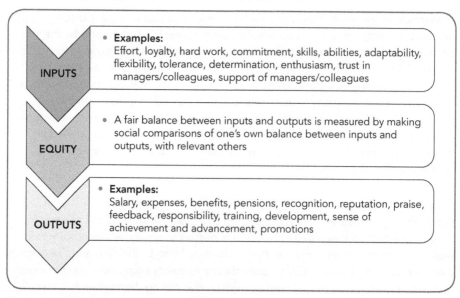

Figure 9.4 Adams' equity theory (1963)

- *Feedback* during the process of working towards goals enables adjustment and maintains focus on goals, giving employees a sense of ownership.
- *Complexity* of goals contributes to motivation, in that challenging but realistic goals result in a greater reward, a valuable sense of achievement and a drive to attain the next goal.

Goal-setting theory has been shown to lead to better performance in organisations, as goals, feedback and rewards give employees an incentive to take ownership of their work and contribute to their organisation. Limitations of this approach refer to goal conflict, in which direction from the organisation, managerial level or personal level may be incompatible. Furthermore, the level of complexity could have a detrimental effect on job performance if goals are perceived to be too complex. If the skills or abilities needed to complete tasks are lacking then employees will become demotivated.

Theories of motivation provide a critical insight into the factors that contribute to employee motivation in organisations. Collectively, theories of motivation demonstrate that basic needs, cognitive processes and goal-directed behaviour perhaps provide the basis for enhancing productivity, performance and job satisfaction. In practice, knowledge of such theories aids our understanding of individual differences in motivation and can facilitate the development of appropriate motivation interventions.

Motivation interventions

For an occupational psychologist, maintaining and promoting motivation is a key element of employee relations. Several interventions to promote and maintain motivation can be identified from key theories, including:

- salary, bonuses, incentives
- appraisal, feedback
- involvement in decision making
- autonomy
- team building
- competencies and goals linked to organisational goals and values.

CASE STUDY

Motivation interventions

A supermarket business on the outskirts of a major UK city needed help with improving the motivation of its employees. The supermarket had a wide range of employees ($n = 32$), consisting of full-time workers ($n = 2$) who had taken early retirement from their lifetime careers; and part-time workers ($n = 30$) including mothers, students and referrals from the local job centre.

Sales had recently been disappointing and staff turnover was high amongst part-time workers. The management team had since sought assistance from an external consultant.

The consultant was able to produce a plan of action for the supermarket based on an initial visit and observation of the work environment; and a questionnaire survey and discussion with the full-time and part-time workers. The following interventions were recommended to the management team at the supermarket to promote motivation amongst employees:

- introduction of a competency-based work book or mutually agreed goals linked to organisational targets
- flexible working hours for part-time workers
- job rotation, to enable employees to gain insight/experience of different departments
- team competition initiatives with rewards for the winning team
- introduction of a bonus/recognition scheme (e.g. 'employee of the month').

Test your knowledge

9.5 What is motivation?

9.6 What are the issues associated with applying needs-based theories of motivation to the workplace?

9.7 How does equity theory compare and contrast with the goal-setting theory of motivation?

9.8 What impact can demotivation have upon employees and organisations?

9.9 Give some examples of interventions that organisations can implement to promote motivation.

Answers to these questions can be found on the companion website at: **www.pearsoned.co.uk/psychologyexpress**.

Further reading

Topic	Key reading
Theories of motivation	Latham, G. P., & Pinder, C. C. (2005). Work motivation theory and research at the dawn of the twenty-first century. *Annual Review of Psychology, 56,* 485–516.
Interventions to promote motivation in organisations	http://www.businessballs.com/motivation

Workplace conflict

Conflict in organisations represents the extent to which an employee or group has negative social interactions with colleagues and co-workers (Jaramillo, Mulki, & Boles, 2011). In general, conflict is associated with negative connotations for employees and organisations. On the other hand, conflict has been described as an inevitable part of dynamic growth (Herriot, 2001). In fact, it is recognised that some conflict can be healthy, as everyday management often involves balancing the interests of different groups. In organisations, it is often a result of negative workplace conflict, when occupational psychologists will be called upon to identify causes behind the breakdown in employee relations. Conflict most frequently arises from a feeling of unfairness, with some of the most common causes including:

- clashes of personality
- different working approaches
- ambiguous organisational structure
- contrasting priorities
- ambiguous relationships.

Workplace conflict can also be linked to theories of motivation as the perception of unfairness resulting in demotivation can also result in negative interactions. Reactions to conflict situations can include anger, resentment, defensiveness and sabotage; all of which can have a detrimental impact on employee performance and wellbeing, as well as strike action or exit from organisations.

Bullying and harassment

Bullying at work occurs when an individual purposefully intimidates or uses aggressive behaviour towards another worker, often in front of colleagues (DirectGov, 2012). Bullying usually, though not always, involves three types of abuse: emotional, verbal and physical (Herriot, 2001). Bullying is similar to harassment; however, this occurs when an individual's behaviour is persistent and offensive – for example, making sexual comments, or abusing an individual's race, religion or sexual orientation (DirectGov, 2012).

Bullying in the workplace can arise from organisational factors: for example, an event or change that allows a shift in power (e.g. restructuring). These are known as precipitating processes as they lead to the occurrence of workplace bullying. Motivating processes, on the other hand, refer to behaviours that literally motivate an individual to continue bullying and using aggressive behaviour. These can arise as a result of the precipitating processes or independently. Finally, enabling processes refer to the systems in place that allow the bullying to continue or go unrecognised (see Figure 9.5).

In addition to this, some individuals may have certain dispositional characteristics that will lead them to engage in bullying behaviour, including:

- *Protection of self-esteem* – the individual feels threatened as a result of distorted self-esteem (e.g. differences in work uniform, or someone having a better desk).
- *Lack of social competencies* – the individual has a lack of emotional control (e.g. poor communication of fear), or a lack of awareness of the impact of their behaviour.

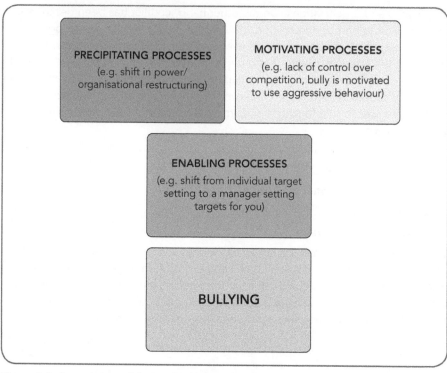

Figure 9.5 Organisational factors leading to bullying

- *Micro-political behaviour* – the individual engages in competitive, assertive and dominant behaviours to 'win' particular situations (e.g. the individual might not be a very good salesperson, in a sales environment).

It is also recognised that certain characteristics may predispose an individual to be a target of bullying and harassment. For example, individuals with a vulnerable personality may lack social skills and be unable to cope effectively in conflict situations. On the other hand, a provocative personality could also predispose an individual to bullying as they may behave in a way that provokes aggressive behaviour from others.

Employee relations and conflict resolution

We have shown that a breakdown in employee relations can lead to negative consequences for both employees and organisations; therefore it is important that the employment relationship is managed and maintained effectively. The work design principle is an approach to managing satisfaction, motivation and performance at work, which suggests that the promotion of employee relations is essentially led from good work/job design (see Figure 9.6).

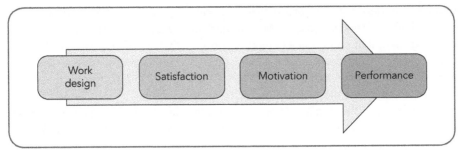

Figure 9.6 **The work design principle**

Employee relations: The term 'employee relations' refers to the regulation of the relationships between employees and employers (Herriot, 2001), both individually and collectively.

Theoretical perspectives of employee relations

There are three main theories of employee relations, each providing a different perspective on the role of conflict, relationships and trade unions. These contrasting perspectives are known as unitarist, neo-unitarist and pluralist (see Table 9.2).

Table 9.2 **Theoretical perspectives of employee relations**

Unitarist	Neo-unitarist	Pluralist
• Organisation is perceived as integrated and harmonious. • Management and employees share common goals. • Teamwork and emphasis on mutual cooperation. • Efforts are made to remove power – everyone is seen as equal. • Refusal to accept conflict exists.	• Organisation is focused on market success. • Emphasis is on human resources rather than senior management. • Efforts are made to develop employees to their full potential. • Training and promotions are available for all employees. • Strict selection procedures.	• Organisation is perceived as being managed by powerful groups. • Management and trade unions hold the balance of power. • Conflict is recognised by the organisation. • Emphasis is on peaceful conflict resolution.

Unitarist and neo-unitarist perspectives are both regarded as extreme views on employee relations. These theories in particular are problematic in terms of recognising that conflict is a natural occurrence that should be expected in the workplace. Both perspectives also suggest that unitarist and neo-unitarist organisations provide no basis for challenge or creativity in an attempt to remove conflict. This ignores the fact that individual employees will be motivated by different factors. The pluralist perspective, on the other hand, acknowledges that conflict can occur and suggests that organisations should have procedures in place to deal with conflict.

Conflict resolution

There are a number of ways in which conflict can be resolved and prevented from occurring in organisations. Conflict resolution can be viewed in relation to two perspectives: collectivism and individualism.

- *Collectivism* refers to collective action. Employees who are united in confronting a conflict situation can be viewed as taking an approach that promotes 'power in numbers'.
- *Individualism* is focused on individual rewards. Individual employees have diverse needs, so the availability of information and legislation on employee rights will empower individuals to take action.

It is suggested that the key factor in the prevention of conflict in organisations is employee involvement (Herriot, 2001). Specifically, employee involvement in organisations promotes empowerment in the workplace. There are several ways to ensure employees are actively involved in decision-making processes in organisations, rather than being instructed to follow orders (see Table 9.3).

Table 9.3 **Employee involvement initiatives**

Employee involvement	Explanation
Employee participation schemes	Employees are given channels whereby they can suggest ideas to managers. Rewards will often be provided for appropriate suggestions.
Focus groups	A group of employees representative of the organisation are asked for their opinions, feedback and suggestions for the organisation.
HR forums	Online space for employees to post questions and share ideas about the organisation.
Quality circles	Employees are delegated responsibility to work on specific tasks or projects.
Performance appraisal	A systematic review process to measure job performance and involve employees in mutual goal setting, discussion and future direction.

Table 9.3 continued

Employee involvement	Explanation
Reward systems	The organisation provides rewards for employee involvement, e.g. rewards for taking part in a focus group or for making appropriate suggestions.
Open-door policies	Managers and directors are visible and interact with employees, e.g. company director visits a shop and works with the sales staff for the day.
Employee surveys	Employees have the opportunity to give anonymous feedback/suggestions to the organisation.

Employee involvement demonstrates that employees are trusted to make decisions for themselves and the organisation. This is also a key motivational tool as employees are often rewarded for their contributions.

Trade unions

Trade unions are independent organisations made up of workers who have come together to represent employees and negotiate specific workplace terms and conditions of employment (Budd & Mumford, 2004). Individuals involved in trade unions often include elected union representatives, human resources departments, MPs and company directors. In order to become a member of a trade union, employees are usually required to contribute a monthly or annual fee to gain access to representation and benefits. Union activities may involve negotiation of pay, working hours, employment contracts, health and safety regulations, occupational benefits, training, equal opportunities and employee welfare. In addition to this, unions are often involved in employment procedures such as redundancies, tribunals and policy making.

In situations of workplace conflict, trade unions will negotiate with organisations on the employees' behalf to reach a mutually agreed solution. Such negotiations do not always reach straightforward agreement, therefore in the past unions have shown support for employees in demonstrations and strike action. In terms of conflict resolution, trade unions provide a democratic system for their members: for example, strike action will be carefully regulated and may take place following a systematic vote or ballot by union members.

Trade unions are not without their limitations. In recent years UK membership has been declining. A possible reason for this is an increase in awareness of employment legislation; therefore employees are more aware of their own rights. Moreover, the economic climate and a decline in the manufacturing industry (the industry most associated with union representation) may also be reflected in a decline in membership.

Further reading

Topic	Key reading
Bullying and harassment	Einarsen, S., Hoel, H., Zapf, D., et al. (2010). *Bullying and harassment in the workplace: Developments in theory, research and practice* (2nd ed.). Boca Raton, FL: CRC Press.
Employee relations	Herriot, P. (2001). *The employment relationship: A psychological perspective*. Hove: Routledge.
Trade unions	Budd, J. W., & Mumford, K. (2004) Trade unions and family-friendly policies in Britain. *Industrial and Labor Relations Review, 57*(2), 204–222.

Chapter summary – pulling it all together

→ Can you tick all the points from the revision checklist at the beginning of this chapter?

→ Attempt the sample question from the beginning of this chapter using the answer guidelines below.

→ Go to the companion website at www.pearsoned.co.uk/psychologyexpress to access more revision support online, including interactive quizzes, flashcards, You be the marker exercises as well as answer guidance for the Test your knowledge and Sample questions from this chapter.

Answer guidelines

 **Sample question**   *Problem-based learning*

You have been asked to consider the factors that led to a breakdown in employee relations in two UK customer service centres that have recently merged. As a result of the merger, the company has closed a major call centre (resulting in several redundancies) and undergone a management restructure.

Several employees who are now based in the new call centre have expressed their anger and dissatisfaction as a result of unfamiliarity with new company procedures and an increased workload. Newly appointed managers are also concerned that their teams appear unhappy and fear that quality of customer service will be affected.

Outline the possible approaches you would take to maintain employee relations at the customer service centre, and provide a clear justification for your recommendations.

Approaching the question

To answer this question, the first thing to consider is how employee relations have been affected with reference to the psychological contract. The question states that issues began to arise after a company merger and management restructure; therefore you will need to familiarise yourself with the range of theories of motivation and workplace conflict and consider the information you need to make recommendations for conflict resolution. For example, were employees informed of the merger and changes to their employment? And how do they feel about their new roles in the new company?

Important points to include

You will need to use a theoretically and practically based justification for your recommendations and approach to maintaining motivation and resolving conflict. For example, if you decide to conduct focus groups with employees, whom would you include in discussions and how would you communicate your findings to the organisation? Then you will need to think about your recommendations. For example, if you choose to recommend a reward scheme or training exercises for employees, then you will need to consider how you would introduce this. Also, what does the literature say about motivation interventions and how can you evaluate their impact on an organisation?

Make your answer stand out

To make your answer stand out, you need to demonstrate an ability to use an evidence base and practical, business knowledge for your decisions. All applied psychologists need to show that they are able to base their recommendations on good science but also demonstrate an awareness of the client they are working with. In this answer it would be beneficial to comment on budget constraints when making your recommendations (due to the initial cost-saving exercise of the company merging with another) and the potential role of trade unions in the conflict resolution.

Explore the accompanying website at www.pearsoned.co.uk/psychologyexpress

→ Prepare more effectively for exams and assignments using the answer guidelines for questions from this chapter.

→ Test your knowledge using multiple choice questions and flashcards.

→ Improve your essay skills by exploring the You be the marker exercises.

Notes

10

Organisational development and change

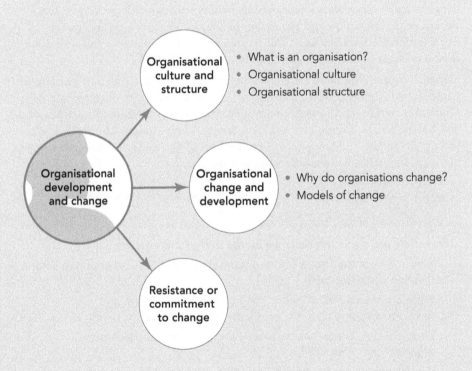

Organisational culture and structure
- What is an organisation?
- Organisational culture
- Organisational structure

Organisational development and change

Organisational change and development
- Why do organisations change?
- Models of change

Resistance or commitment to change

A printable version of this topic map is available from
www.pearsoned.co.uk/psychologyexpress

Introduction

Organisations can be defined as a social group of individuals, systematically structured and managed to meet needs or pursue collective goals on a continuous basis (Chapman, 2012). Often made up of a variety of different structures, management structures in organisations are specifically set up to govern relationships and responsibilities between employees. It is also important to remember that as well as involving internal activity, organisations are open systems that can affect and can be affected by wider society and the environment.

Organisational development is a planned effort to increase an organisation's effectiveness and facilitate change, based on scientific research and theory (CIPD, 2012). Organisational development is supported by promoting commitment from employees and stakeholders. Organisational development consultancy in occupational psychology involves problem diagnosis and the design, implementation and evaluation of solutions focused on improving organisational effectiveness and/or improving an organisation's ability to cope during periods of change or development (Millward, 2005).

Depending upon the need for change in organisations, the role of occupational psychologists in this process is to support an organisation in developing a new vision and culture, and to help the organisation to review structures, processes and behaviours to identify barriers to success. A key aspect of this role is also to help managers and leaders to communicate effectively and demonstrate the interpersonal skills necessary to carry out the change.

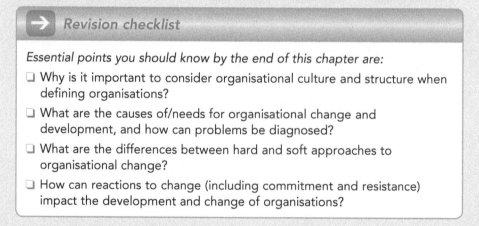

→ Revision checklist

Essential points you should know by the end of this chapter are:

❏ Why is it important to consider organisational culture and structure when defining organisations?

❏ What are the causes of/needs for organisational change and development, and how can problems be diagnosed?

❏ What are the differences between hard and soft approaches to organisational change?

❏ How can reactions to change (including commitment and resistance) impact the development and change of organisations?

Assessment advice

Assessment questions on this topic are likely to take the form of either an essay-based question or a problem-based learning task. Whichever form of assessment you complete on this topic, it is important to remember that there are many factors that influence organisational development and change beyond those covered in this chapter. Good answers to either type of question will draw upon issues covered in other chapters in this revision guide.

Typical *essay questions* on this topic will require you to be evidence-based in your answers, by considering theoretical, research and practical issues surrounding this topic. You will need to think about how theories of organisational culture and structure are important to diagnosing problems or identifying the need for organisational change. For example, you may be asked to critically evaluate the nature of organisational problems (hard or soft), and how this can impact upon employees.

Problem-based questions in occupational psychology often take the form of a case study that will require you to apply your understanding and creativity based on the topics covered in this chapter. You will need to think critically about how to address issues including resistance to change, in order to make recommendations for gaining employee commitment during organisational development.

Sample question

Could you answer this question? Below is a typical problem question that could arise on this topic.

 Sample question   *Problem-based learning*

A chain of retail organisations recently introduced a new set of company values in response to customer feedback and a decrease in sales figures. The new values were communicated effectively and seemed to be welcomed enthusiastically by front-line employees. Following email communication from head office, store managers were instructed to disseminate the following message to front-line employees. 'This is where we want to be in 12 months' time to ensure we are driving sales, meeting customer needs and exceeding the performance of our competitors. You will all be monitored on achieving our new company values in your day-to-day work.'

Despite the initial enthusiasm and willingness to engage with new values, 6 weeks later store managers started to notice lack of motivation and lower productivity. When questioned, some employees had started to feel resentful of the new values as a lot of the new procedures were perceived to be the same as before. Employees specifically expressed dissatisfaction as a result of 'being told to do something we were doing well in the first place'.

Based on your knowledge of organisational change, critically consider what steps the organisation should take in the light of the current circumstances. Provide a justification for your recommendations for how the organisation can move forward.

Guidelines on answering this question are included at the end of this chapter, whilst guidance on tackling other exam questions can be found on the companion website at **www.pearsoned.co.uk/psychologyexpress**

Organisational culture and structure

What is an organisation?

Organisations are social activity systems that are designed, structured and coordinated to achieve goals (Daft, Murphy, & Willmott, 2010). Goals and outcomes of organisations will vary enormously across different industries and sectors; however, the underlying general purpose of organisations is largely based on the same principles. For example, organisations bring together resources to achieve desired goals and outcomes; produce goods and services efficiently; facilitate innovation; use modern manufacturing, service and information technologies; adapt to and influence changing environments; create value for owners, customers and employees; and accommodate ongoing challenges of diversity, ethics, and the motivation and coordination of employees (Daft, Murphy, & Willmott, 2010).

In addition to this, organisations can be described as open or closed systems. Most commonly, organisations adopt an open system approach in which they continuously interact with and adapt to the wider environment (Senior & Swailes, 2010). On the other hand, a closed system organisation remains isolated from the outside environment: for example, a production is often kept separate from external elements, including executive meetings and information from other similar/competitor production lines.

It is important for us as occupational psychologists to remember that organisations are made up of formal and informal factors. Formal factors refer to the visible part of organisations, such as structures, strategies, goals, products and physical resources. In contrast, factors such as culture, attitudes and values are often referred to as the informal factors in an organisation. The metaphor of the 'organisational iceberg' helps to illustrate this, depicting two contrasting sides of organisations (Senior & Swailes, 2010) (see Figure 10.1).

The formal aspects shown above the water are thought of as 'easy to see and measure', especially when considering organisational change, for example. However, informal aspects such as organisational culture are not only unseen, but also make up the larger part of organisations. For example, behavioural norms, culture, values and attitudes within an organisation will often influence the formal aspects in terms of management, decision making and actions. Therefore, in consultancy it is important to assess these informal factors, as they are often the most influential factors determining how an organisation will handle change.

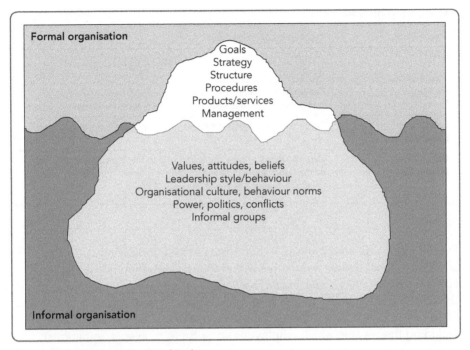

Figure 10.1 The organisational iceberg
Source: Adapted from *Organizational Change*, Senior, B., and Swailes, S., Pearson Education Limited © Barbara Senior and Stephen Swailes 2010

Organisational culture

Organisational culture refers to the governing philosophy of the organisation, within which underlying values are expressed. The culture of an organisation has been described as the shared meanings, values, and beliefs that are created and communicated within an organisation (Ashkanasy, Wilderom, & Peterson, 2000), and is closely linked to the development of employee relations (see Chapter 9). At the organisational level, a company mission or vision statement will often convey a strong message about the purpose and values of an organisation, and acts as a guide for all organisational activity (see Table 10.1). Different industries and sectors therefore adopt a variety of cultural typologies, each focusing on a variety of different values and goals (Burke, Borucki, & Kaufman, 2002). For example, emergency services' values and culture are often based on the protection of life; the financial industry often emphasises a 'work hard, play hard' culture; and the social services sector is usually focused on people-oriented values.

Table 10.1 Examples of vision/mission statements in organisations

Organisation	Vision/mission statement
GlaxoSmithKline	At GSK our mission is to improve the quality of human life by enabling people to do more, feel better and live longer.

Table 10.1 **continued**

Organisation	Vision/mission statement
Nike	To bring inspiration and innovation to every athlete* in the world.
Facebook	Facebook's mission is to give people the power to share and make the world more open and connected. (Facebook, 2012)
Sainsbury's Supermarkets	To be the most trusted retailer, where people love to work and shop.
British Heart Foundation	Our mission is to play a leading role in the fight against disease of the heart and circulation so that it is no longer a major cause of disability and premature death.

Everything inside an organisation contributes to its underlying culture, showing values, beliefs and norms within that organisation. Organisational culture is generally a shared set of assumptions, understandings and norms that current employees will teach to new starters (Daft, Murphy, & Wilmott, 2010). For example, different organisations may have certain traditions, including the ways in which employees socialise (e.g. events, initiations); popular stories about the organisation that are passed on to new employees; and symbols/logos on display in the organisation, to name but a few. During this entry process, new employees adjust to the organisational environment, which also helps to build the psychological contract (De Vos and Freese, 2011). To illustrate this, Johnson, Scholes, and Whittington (2008) identified a web of organisational culture, outlining factors that contribute to the patterned ways of thinking and behaving in organisations (see Figure 10.2).

Culture is therefore a lens through which an organisation can be understood and interpreted (Parmelli et al., 2011). However, culture should refer not only to organisational values but also to principles and standards regarding behaviour (Rahmati, Darouian, & Ahmadinia, 2012). This raises the question of whose values are to be employed in determining standards and other related issues when individuals are required to exercise judgement.

Organisational structure

Structure in an organisation refers to the arrangements by which activities and duties are coordinated and managed for the purpose of achieving organisational goals (Rahmati, Darouian, & Ahmadinia, 2012). The structure of an organisation consists of activities such as delegation of tasks involving collaboration, coordination and management, which are directed towards the achievement of the aims of the organisation. In this respect, whilst

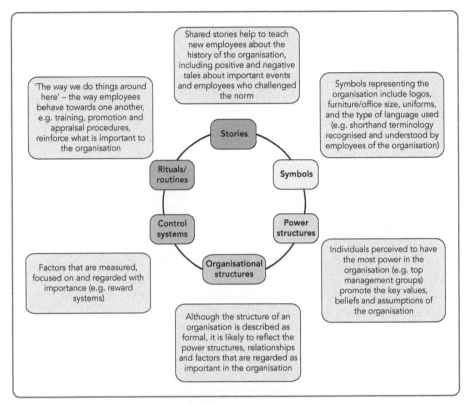

The way we do things around here' – the way employees behave towards one another, e.g. training, promotion and appraisal procedures, reinforce what is important to the organisation

Shared stories help to teach new employees about the history of the organisation, including positive and negative tales about important events and employees who challenged the norm

Symbols representing the organisation include logos, furniture/office size, uniforms, and the type of language used (e.g. shorthand terminology recognised and understood by employees of the organisation)

Stories

Rituals/ routines

Symbols

Control systems

Power structures

Organisational structures

Factors that are measured, focused on and regarded with importance (e.g. reward systems)

Individuals perceived to have the most power in the organisation (e.g. top management groups) promote the key values, beliefs and assumptions of the organisation

Although the structure of an organisation is described as formal, it is likely to reflect the power structures, relationships and factors that are regarded as important in the organisation

Figure 10.2 **Web of organisational culture**

structure is described as a formal aspect of organisations, it is closely related to the informal culture. Formal and informal organisational structures are interdependent entities that contribute to the firm's working environment, reflecting relationships between departments, divisions and teams, for example (Sellitto, 2011). The formal organisational structure is observable and perhaps more easily understood, whereas informal networks are, by definition, difficult to identify (Sellito, 2011). Organisational structure fosters interpersonal relationships, levels of control and pathways of communication, which provides a clear understanding of who and where employees can turn to under different circumstances (Senior & Swailes, 2010).

Most commonly, organisational structure is represented in the form of a hierarchical pyramid, outlining key roles and levels within an organisation. For example, Figure 10.3 shows a mock organisation with six hierarchical levels, with the tip of the pyramid highlighting the Chief Executive Officer (CEO) or Managing Director (MD) at the top of the organisation, and the majority of employees included in the broader levels of the organisation at the base of the pyramid.

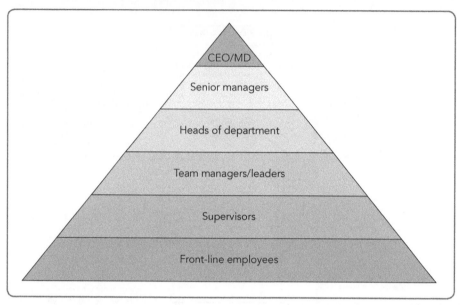

Figure 10.3 **An example of a hierarchical organisational structure**

However, hierarchy is not the only defining feature of organisational structure. Robbins and Barnwell (2006) identified three key dimensions of structure: formalisation, centralisation and complexity (see Table 10.2). These dimensions enable occupational psychologists to understand and compare organisations based on key aspects of structure: for example, does the organisation have a hierarchy in place; how does the decision-making process work; and how are different job roles and departments defined?

In the light of this, it is important to recognise that structure will differ considerably between different types of organisation according to origin/history, size, culture, location and purpose. In particular, choices about structure should not be based on the preferences of senior managers, but on the needs and goals of the organisation (Woods & West, 2010). For example, variations of the above components can lead to mechanistic or organic structures.

● *Mechanistic* (e.g. councils, government, universities). These structures are characterised by high levels of complexity, formalisation and centralisation; considerable division of labour; heavy reliance on formal rules; well-established/traditional career paths; and a clearly defined hierarchy.

● *Organic* (e.g. marketing firms, Ministry of Defence special units). These are characterised by low levels of complexity and formalisation; decentralisation of decision making; flexibility of labour; adaptability to rules and regulations; organisation around unique problems/tasks; and diverse professional skills.

Mechanistic and organic structures can impact organisational behaviour over time. Specifically, large mechanistic organisations often harbour formal

Table 10.2 Dimensions of organisational structure

Dimensions	Explanation	Advantages	Disadvantages
Formalisation	The degree to which various activities, rules, procedures and instructions are defined and standardised in an organisation (e.g. Is there a hierarchy? How formal is it? Does communication work both ways?)	+ Reduces the unpredictability in the organisation as activities are standardised. + Activities are defined, leading to effective coordination between managers and subordinates. + Decisions are made on the basis of standard rules and procedures. + Standardised activity reduces conflict and ambiguity.	− Limited creativity and flexibility in the organisation as most activities are standardised. − Difficult to change the standardised procedures in the organisation.
Centralisation	The degree to which decision-making is centralised in the organisation. In centralisation, decisions are made by the top-level management. In contrast, decentralisation works in the opposite way, involving the delegation of power to the lower levels of the organisation.	+ Beneficial for small organisations with informal structure (e.g. the business owner is responsible for decision making).	− Impossible to have absolute centralisation in larger organisations due to size, interdependence of work-flow, complexity of activities and physical/informal barriers between groups.
Complexity	Refers to the differences amongst job roles and departments. Therefore, complexity shows the degree of differentiation within the organisation.	+ Shows the degree of coordination, communication and control within the organisation.	− Increased complexity can make management quite difficult.

hierarchical structuring of relationships, whereas organic organisations tend to be less formal. In this respect, the underlying values and culture of an organisation that apply to all employees are the foundation of the overt and covert behaviours and relationships of all individuals who work within an organisation.

Test your knowledge

10.1 What is an organisation?

10.2 What are the key differences between formal and informal aspects of organisations?

10.3 Explain how organisational culture might be linked to employee relations.

10.4 Why is organisational structure important to the maintenance of relationships in organisations?

Answers to these questions can be found on the companion website at: **www.pearsoned.co.uk/psychologyexpress.**

Further reading

Topic	Key reading
Organisational culture and structure	Ashkanasy, N. M., Wilderom, C. P. M., & Peterson, M. F. (2000). *Handbook of organizational culture and climate.* London: Sage.
	Senior, B., & Swailes, S. (2010). *Organizational change* (4th ed.). Harlow: Prentice Hall.
Organisational culture (linked to employee relations)	Evans, S. (2012). Analysis of the relationship that exists between organizational culture, motivation and performance. *Problems of Management in the 21st Century, 3,* 106–119.
	Hui-Min, K. (2009). Understanding relationships between academic staff and administrators: An organizational culture perspective. *Journal of Higher Education Policy and Management, 31*(1), 43–54.

Organisational change and development

Why do organisations change?

Organisational change has been defined as the alterations of existing work routines and strategies that affect a whole organisation (Herold, Fedor, & Caldwell, 2007). Over time, organisations may change their focus, expand or contract their activities or rethink their products and services (CIPD, 2012). Therefore, for the occupational psychologist it is often apparent that more established organisations, for example, often look nothing like they used to, in response to a number of factors.

Such factors can be described as *external* or *internal triggers*, both leading to the need for change in organisations (see Table 10.3). As the name implies, external

Table 10.3 Internal and external triggers of organisational change

External triggers of change (PEST)

- Political – e.g. changes in government legislation and initiatives
- Economic – e.g. challenge of economic downturn and tougher trading climates
- Sociocultural – e.g. impact of an ageing workforce
- Technological – e.g. use of smartphones/advanced computer technology in place of shorthand

Internal triggers of change

- Decision making – e.g. centralisation
- Organisational hierarchy – e.g. new senior manager
- Degree of formalisation – e.g. new marketing strategy/new organisational policy

factors affect the organisation from the outside or above the organisational structure. For example, changes to government policy, advances in technological systems, the economic climate, and so on, can have a considerable impact on all types of organisation. Such Political, Economic, Sociocultural and Technological factors are known as PEST triggers. On the other hand, triggers of change can also be identified from within an organisation: for example, the introduction of a new manager or structure, or a new company policy.

CASE STUDY

Consequences of 'poor' organisational structure

It is important to point out that there are no specific good or bad organisational structures per se, as different organisations have different needs. But the structure and environment of an organisation should determine and support the organisation to achieve its specific goals; therefore structure can be deemed inappropriate or poor if it fails to do this.

Several consequences of 'poor' organisational structure were identified at a customer services call centre in the southwest of England, based on work by Furnham (2005).

Following an independent report from an occupational psychologist, it was identified that decision making regarding delegation, staff development and procedures in the call centre was often late and inappropriate. In particular, there was a major lack of relevant and timely information provided to employees, and decision making was poorly coordinated between individuals based in different departments. As decision making was not centralised, several (but not all) supervisors had been appointed as decision-makers and were experiencing work-overload due to poor delegation. In addition to this, a survey of employees suggested that it was not clear who the decision-makers were, resulting in ambiguity about whom to go to in the event of a problem or where to get key information from. It was also apparent that there had been a lack of evaluation of the outcome of past decisions, resulting in poor knowledge of staff needs and appropriate procedures, all of which contributed to a vicious cycle of inappropriate decision making.

As a result of this, the employee survey suggested that morale and motivation were low amongst employees in the call centre, as a result of inconsistent, limited information and poor decision making (particularly surrounding delegation of work). Overall, job definitions and performance assessment were ambiguous for most employees and there was a general lack of support systems in place.

In line with Johns (1992), the call centre presented several of the five major symptoms of structural problems:

- poor job design
- ambiguity of job roles
- inter- and intra-departmental conflict
- slow decision making and response times
- decision making on incomplete or insufficient information with lack of evaluation.

As a result of the independent review, it was suggested that the organisational structure showed the need for change within the call centre as a result of internal triggers.

Models of change

Change management has been approached from different perspectives, based on theoretical predictions and preferences of academic and consultant practitioners (Mathews, 2009). *Episodic* and *continuous* models of change refer to contrasting viewpoints on intermittent and planned action versus constant, ever-evolving change (Weick and Quinn, 1999). Episodic change is described as an occasional interruption from the norm as a result of an external trigger, which brings an organisation to a new equilibrium, until the next perceived need for another change process (Cameron & Green, 2012). On the other hand, continuous change refers to a normal characteristic of working life, rather than a single episode of upheaval, driven by an awareness of daily contingencies (Weick & Quinn, 1999). Alternatively, the *systems* perspective of change suggests that organisations are made up of a number of dynamic sub-systems, so a change in one sub-system will effect change in other related systems (Woods & West, 2010). An example of a systems model of change is the McKinsey 7S model, which identified a framework of seven independent systems in organisations that can be used in the analysis of change (see Figure 10.4).

A critique of the model, however, points out that the framework does not account for external factors that may influence change.

'Hard' or 'soft' problems?

Depending on the context of the need for change within an organisation, *what* needs to change and *how* the change should be implemented may

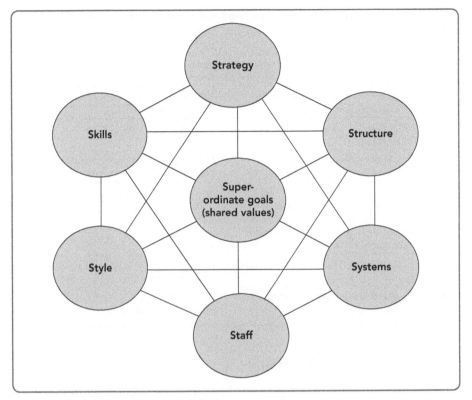

Figure 10.4 **The McKinsey 7S model**

or may not be clear; therefore change can be defined as a type of *problem* (Senior & Swailes, 2010). Problems that lead to change in organisations are often identified as either 'hard' or 'soft'.

Hard problems tend to occur on a smaller scale and are associated with getting an organisation from its present state to an agreed future position. In this respect, hard problems are distinctive for having clear priorities, and objectives to achieve the change are generally quantifiable to enable assessment: for example, the introduction of a new till system in a retail organisation. On the other hand, a soft problem has no clear measurement of success and tends to have a wider impact on the organisation as a whole: for example, low morale and motivation or high turnover and absenteeism amongst employees. A soft problem can have a 'ripple effect' and spread throughout an organisation. Soft problems therefore result in conflicts of interest and differences in opinions regarding their solution.

It is important to note that the terms 'hard' and 'soft' do not refer to the difficulty of the change. In fact, hard problems are often associated with material or physical assets and soft problems often involve people. Hard and soft problems are therefore defined by their differing characteristics, including Timescales, Resources, Objectives, Perceptions, Interest, Control and Source, known as the TROPICS factors (see Table 10.4).

Table 10.4 The TROPICS factors of hard and soft organisational problems

	Hard	Soft
T	Timescales clearly defined (short–medium term)	Timescales ill defined (medium–long term)
R	Resources needed for the change clearly identified	Resources needed for the change uncertain (ripple effect)
O	Objectives are clearly stated and quantifiable	Objectives are subjective and ambiguous
P	Perceptions of the problem and possible solutions are shared by all	No consensus on what constitutes the problem/conflict of interest
I	Interest in the problem is limited and defined (e.g. only affects certain people – a change in the Humanities department of a university does not necessarily affect the Business School)	Interest in the problem is widespread and ill defined
C	Control is maintained by the managing group	Control is shared with people outside the managing group
S	Source of the problem originates from within the organisation	Source of the problem originates from outside the organisation

Hard systems model of change

The hard systems model of change is a method of designing and managing change that follows a three-phase process with emphasis placed on setting goals/objectives, developing a plan of action and measuring achievement.

1 *Definition phase* – describing/diagnosing the problem; setting goals to determine the success criteria; and identifying the performance indicators (measuring the progress from A to B): for example, e.g. high volume of items stolen from a retail store (baseline measure taken) – loss prevention strategy required.

2 *Evaluation phase* – generating a plan of action for the change; selecting appropriate methods to evaluate progress: for example, CCTV installed, staff training in loss prevention, improved store layout and visual merchandising.

3 *Implementation phase* – putting the plan of action into practice and monitoring the outcome: for example, monitoring of number of items stolen over a set period of time (e.g. 6 months) to enable comparison with the baseline measure.

In order for hard systems of change to be successful, the support of senior managers is needed as well as the involvement of those employees affected by the change. If employees are informed of the process as early as possible, they will take ownership of the change and will be less likely to resist.

Most importantly, if there is no way of measuring performance indicators when working towards the solution of an organisational problem, it is *not* a hard change.

Soft systems model of change

Soft problems within organisations are more intricate than hard problems, so it is not often possible to define one single solution. The consequence of this is that the design of change in 'messy' situations needs to account for issues such as problem ownership, communication, and the participation and commitment of people involved in the change process (Cameron & Green, 2012). The organisational development process refers to the process of facilitation of organisational change and renewal (Senior & Swailes, 2010). One of the best-known organisational development models of planned change is Lewin's (1951) three-phase process of unfreezing, moving and refreezing.

1 *Unfreezing* involves the preparation of the organisation for change, which requires a disruption of the status quo within the organisation in order to build a new way of operating. Attitudes, beliefs, values and behaviours need to be challenged in order to build motivation to seek a new equilibrium. Use employee attitude surveys, focus groups, direct observations and reviews of organisations records.

2 *Moving* – over time employees begin to behave in ways that support the new direction, once they buy in to how the change will affect them. Involve employees in decision making and encourage engagement in the change process, gain employee feedback and consult rather than inform.

3 *Refreezing* involves stabilising the changes to ensure they become the norm within the organisation. Ensure employees feel comfortable with new ways of working, and introduce praise or reward for taking on the change, training and development.

CRITICAL FOCUS

Application of Lewin's (1951) model of planned change

In practice, Lewin's (1951) model of planned change is rather simplistic and suggests that soft systems of change can follow a single linear process of preparation, behaviour/ attitude change of employees and standardisation of new ways of working. However, soft problems are described as widespread, often the result of a ripple effect, and face difficulties of differing perspectives and opinions of people with regard to course of action and solutions. It is therefore important to recognise that in practice, organisational development is often a continuous process that sometimes requires steps of the model to be revisited: for example, gaining commitment to the change is not necessarily a standalone phase and requires attention throughout the change. Similarly, during the 'refreeze', it may be necessary to revisit the future vision and revise the action plan, depending on the outcome of the evaluation. It could also be argued that organisations may never reach a stable state at which they can be 'unfrozen'. In this case, it is questionable whether managers can ever have sufficient information to plan change fully from the start.

In contrast to the assumptions of hard systems of change that tend to follow a loop of phases, soft systems of change should recognise the complexity of changing the behaviour of people, which Lewin's model does not necessarily account for.

More recently, the organisational development model of change has developed to reflect the complexity of the process (Senior & Fleming, 2006) (see Figure 10.5). This model specifically recognises that the change can go backwards and forwards to iterate the process, and organisations can potentially change during the process, requiring managers or individuals involved in facilitating the change to revisit steps of the model.

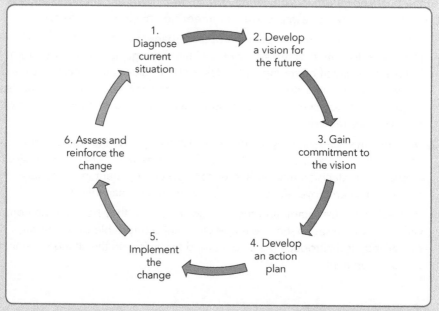

Figure 10.5 Organisational development model of change
Source: Adapted from *Organisational Change*, Senior, B., and Fleming, J., Pearson Education Limited © Barbara Senior and Jocelyn Fleming 2006

Test your knowledge

10.5 Give some examples of external factors (such as PEST) and how they trigger the need for change.

10.6 What are the research methods you could implement to diagnose problems in organisations?

10.7 Describe in detail three key differences between hard and soft organisational problems.

10.8 What are the strengths and weaknesses of Lewin's (1951) model of planned change in organisations?

Answers to these questions can be found on the companion website at: www.pearsoned.co.uk/psychologyexpress.

Further reading

Topic	Key reading
Organisational change and development	Cameron, E., & Green, M. (2012). *Making sense of change management* (3rd ed.). London: Kogan Page.
	Parumasur, S. B. (2012). The effect of organisational context on organisational development (OD) interventions. *South African Journal of Industrial Psychology, 38*(1), 1–12.
	Rusaw, A. C. (2007). Changing public organizations: Four approaches. *International Journal of Public Administration, 30,* 347–361.
	Smith, I. (2010). Organisational quality and organisational change: Interconnecting paths to effectiveness. *Organisational Quality and Change 32*(1/2), 111–128.
Systems of change	Mathews, J. (2009). Models of change management: A reanalysis. *Journal of Business Strategy, 4*(2), 7–17.

Resistance or commitment to change

It has been estimated that as many as 50 per cent of changes in organisations fail to meet their intended objectives or outcomes (Marks, 2006). Factors that contribute to the success or failure of change have been attributed to sources at the organisational and employee level. It has been suggested that employees' attitudes and behaviours play a major role in the success or failure of change (Shin, Taylor, & Seo, 2012). How employees react to change, whether that be positively or negatively, can have key implications for the overall change process.

It is quite common for some change to be welcomed by employees: for example, new green policies or schemes to improve customer satisfaction are often perceived positively, and employees willingly engage in new activity (Woods & West, 2010). Creating a committed workforce in the midst of change has become one of the highest priorities in the field of human resource management (Swailes, 2004). Therefore, a key focus on gaining commitment from employees from the start of the change process should be factored into the planned change. Meyer and Herscovitch (2001) proposed a Three-Component Model (TCM) of organisational commitment which suggests employees are categorised by different mindsets that determine their commitment to change.

1 *Affective component* – employees' emotional attachment to, and desire to remain engaged with, the organisation.

2 *Normative component* – employees' perceived obligation to remain engaged with the organisation.

3 *Continuance component* – employees' perceived costs of disengaging with the organisation.

The TCM argues that employees can have different levels of commitment based on combinations of the three components, creating a 'commitment profile' that demonstrates behavioural support for organisational change. However, little is yet known about potential predictors of employees' organisational commitment. Machin, Fogharty, and Bannon (2009) conducted an exploratory study of employee commitment to change in the Australian public sector. It was found that organisational climate (employee perceptions of the work environment) were significant predictors of behavioural support for change. Specifically, a positive work environment was a significant predictor of all three components of commitment, whereas a negative work environment predicted only the continuance component and was negatively related to behavioural support for change.

On the other hand, resistance to organisational change has been described as a negative reaction and can occur at the organisational or employee level in response to several different factors (Woods & West, 2010). Individual sources of resistance can occur for several different reasons, including selective perception, habit, inconvenience or loss of freedom, economic implications, job security/past experience, or fear of the unknown/uncertainty (Mullins, 2007). Moreover, resistance can occur from organisational sources, such as culture, a focus on maintaining stability, investment in resources, past contracts or agreements, or threats to power/influence. In addition to the model of planned change, Lewin (1951) developed a forcefield analysis of change, encompassing the idea that organisations maintain an equilibrium that is held in place by two sets of forces – forces that drive the change forwards and resisting forces that hold the change back (see Figure 10.6).

The forcefield analysis demonstrates that for change to happen, the driving forces have to outweigh the resisting forces. Therefore, planned change strategies that are managed effectively will ensure the driving and resisting forces are rebalanced to maintain organisational equilibrium following the change. Thus,

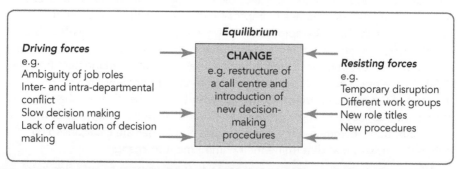

Figure 10.6 Organisational development model of change
Source: Adapted from *Organizational Change*, Senior, B., and Swailes, S., Pearson Education Limited © Barbara Senior and Stephen Swailes 2010

a key factor in planning effective change is gaining and maintaining commitment and support from employees. In order to promote this, effective communication is essential to keep employees informed from the initial planning stages of the change. Therefore, an appropriate organisational structure with clear communication pathways will be effective in nurturing this process, in addition to the research methods discussed above to gain feedback.

Test your knowledge

10.9 Give some examples of factors that lead some individual employees to resist change.

10.10 Describe what is meant by organisational equilibrium.

10.11 Explain the differences between the three components of commitment to change, according to Meyer and Herscovitch (2001).

Answers to these questions can be found on the companion website at: www.pearsoned.co.uk/psychologyexpress.

Further reading

Topic	Key reading
Resistance to change	Shin, J., Taylor, M. S., & Seo, M-G. (2012). Resources for change: The real relationships of organizational inducements and psychological resilience to employees' attitudes and behaviors toward organizational change. *Academy of Management Journal, 55*(3), 727–748.
Commitment to change	Swailes, S. (2004) Commitment to change: Profiles of commitment and in-role performance. *Personnel Review, 33,* 187–204.

Chapter summary – pulling it all together

→ Can you tick all the points from the revision checklist at the beginning of this chapter?

→ Attempt the sample question from the beginning of this chapter using the answer guidelines below.

→ Go to the companion website at www.pearsoned.co.uk/psychologyexpress to access more revision support online, including interactive quizzes, flashcards, You be the marker exercises as well as answer guidance for the Test your knowledge and Sample questions from this chapter.

Answer guidelines

Sample question   *Problem-based learning*

A chain of retail organisations recently introduced a new set of company values in response to customer feedback and a decrease in sales figures. The new values were communicated effectively and seemed to be welcomed enthusiastically by front-line employees. Following email communication from head office, store managers were instructed to disseminate the following message to front-line employees. 'This is where we want to be in 12 months' time to ensure we are driving sales, meeting customer needs and exceeding the performance of our competitors. You will all be monitored on achieving our new company values in your day-to-day work.'

Despite the initial enthusiasm and willingness to engage with new values, 6 weeks later store managers started to notice lack of motivation and lower productivity. When questioned, some employees had started to feel resentful of the new values as a lot of the new procedures were perceived to be the same as before. Employees specifically expressed dissatisfaction as a result of 'being told to do something we were doing well in the first place'.

Based on your knowledge of organisational change, critically consider what steps the organisation should take in the light of the current circumstances. Provide a justification for your recommendations for how the organisation can move forward.

Approaching the question

To answer this question, the first thing to consider is organisational culture and structure. The question states that issues began to arise only after specific email communication from head office, despite initial enthusiasm for a new set of values for the company. Therefore you will need to consider organisational structure and communication and how this may have contributed to employee dissatisfaction and resistance to the change. For example, how were employees informed of the need for changing company values? Were they initially told that their performance would be monitored? Have they lost their sense of ownership of the change? Think about how this relates to a violation of the psychological contract. It is also important to consider the factors that led the organisation to change its values in the first instance. You will need to familiarise yourself with the theories/ models of change to explore whether changing company values in response to customer feedback and poor sales figures was the most appropriate step to take. What would you have done differently if you had designed the change process?

Important points to include

You will need to use a theoretically and practically based justification for your recommendations and approach to diagnosing the problem (hard or soft?) and designing a change process. For example, if you decide to conduct a survey of employees, whom would you include and how would you use your findings to plan the change? Then you will need to think about your recommendations. For example, when would be a good time to 'unfreeze'? If you choose to recommend a planned change, then you will need to consider a timescale to revisit certain steps in the cycle. Also, what does the literature say about the importance of communication and gaining commitment for the change? Is the structure of the organisation appropriate to allow the change to happen?

Make your answer stand out

To make your answer stand out, you need to demonstrate an ability to use an evidence base and practical, business knowledge for your decisions. All applied psychologists need to show that they are able to base their recommendations on good science, but also demonstrate an awareness of the client they are working with. In this answer it would be beneficial to comment on the psychological contract (draw on your knowledge of employee relations), organisational and individual sources of resistance, and the potential ways in which you can gain and maintain commitment and behavioural support for the change.

Explore the accompanying website at **www.pearsoned.co.uk/psychologyexpress**

→ Prepare more effectively for exams and assignments using the answer guidelines for questions from this chapter.
→ Test your knowledge using multiple choice questions and flashcards.
→ Improve your essay skills by exploring the You be the marker exercises.

Notes

Notes

And finally, before the exam . . .

How to approach revision from here

You should now be at a reasonable stage in your revision process – you should have developed your skills and knowledge base over your course and used this text judiciously during that period. Now, however, you have used the book to reflect on, remind yourself of and reinforce the material you have researched over the year/seminar. You will, of course, need to do additional reading and research to that included here (and appropriate directions are provided) but you will be well on your way with the material presented in this book.

It is important that in answering any question in psychology you take a research- and evidence-based approach to your response. For example, do not make generalised or sweeping statements that cannot be substantiated or supported by evidence from the literature. Remember as well that the evidence should not be anecdotal – it is of no use citing your mum, dad, best friend or the latest news from a celebrity website. After all, you are not writing an opinion piece – you are crafting an argument that is based on current scientific knowledge and understanding. You need to be careful about the evidence you present: do review the material and from where it was sourced.

Furthermore, whatever type of assessment you have to undertake, it is important to take an evaluative approach to the evidence. Whether you are writing an essay, sitting an exam or designing a webpage, the key advice is to avoid simply presenting a descriptive answer. Rather, it is necessary to think about the strength of the evidence in each area. One of the key skills for psychology students is critical thinking and for this reason the tasks featured in this series focus upon developing this way of thinking. Thus you are not expected to simply learn a set of facts and figures, but to think about the implications of what we know and how this might be applied in everyday life. The best assessment answers are the ones that take this critical approach.

It is also important to note that psychology is a theoretical subject: when answering any question about psychology, not only refer to the prevailing theories of the field, but outline the development of them as well. It is also important to evaluate these theories and models either through comparison with other models and theories or through the use of studies that have assessed them and highlighted their strengths and weaknesses. It is essential to read widely – within each section of this book there are directions to interesting and pertinent papers relating to the specific topic area. Find these papers, read these papers and make notes from these papers. But don't stop there. Let them lead you to other sources that may be important to the field. One thing that an examiner hates to see is the same old sources being cited all of the time: be innovative and, as well as reading the seminal works, find the more obscure and interesting sources too – just make sure they're relevant to your answer!

How not to revise

- **Don't avoid revision.** This is the best tip ever. There is something on the TV, the pub is having a two-for-one offer, the fridge needs cleaning, your budgie looks lonely . . . You have all of these activities to do and they need doing now! Really . . .? Do some revision!
- **Don't spend too long at each revision session.** Working all day and night is not the answer to revision. You do need to take breaks, so schedule your revision so you are not working from dawn until dusk. A break gives time for the information you have been revising to consolidate.
- **Don't worry.** Worrying will cause you to lose sleep, lose concentration and lose revision time by leaving it late and then later. When the exam comes, you will have no revision completed and will be tired and confused.
- **Don't cram.** This is the worst revision technique in the universe! You will not remember the majority of the information that you try to stuff into your skull, so why bother?
- **Don't read over old notes with no plan.** Your brain will take nothing in. If you wrote your lecture notes in September and the exam is in May, is there any point in trying to decipher your scrawly handwriting now?
- **Don't write model answers and learn by rote.** When it comes to the exam you will simply regurgitate the model answer irrespective of the question – not a brilliant way to impress the examiner!

Tips for exam success

What you should do when it comes to revision

Exams are one form of assessment that students often worry about the most. The key to exam success, as with many other types of assessment, lies in good preparation and self-organisation. One of the most important things is knowing what to expect – this does not necessarily mean knowing what the questions will be on the exam paper, but rather what the structure of the paper is, how many questions you are expected to answer, how long the exam will last and so on.

To pass an exam you need a good grasp of the course material and, obvious as it may seem, to turn up for the exam itself. It is important to remember that you aren't expected to know or remember everything in the course, but you should be able to show your understanding of what you have studied. Remember as well that examiners are interested in what you know, not what you don't know.

They try to write exam questions that give you a good chance of passing – not ones to catch you out or trick you in any way. You may want to consider some of these top exam tips.

- Start your revision in plenty of time.
- Make a revision timetable and stick to it.
- Practise jotting down answers and making essay plans.
- Practise writing against the clock using past exam papers.
- Check that you have really answered the question and have not strayed off the point.
- Review a recent past paper and check the marking structure.
- Carefully select the topics you are going to revise.
- Use your lecture/study notes and refine them further, if possible, into lists or diagrams and transfer them on to index cards/Post-it notes. Mind maps are a good way of making links between topics and ideas.
- Practise your handwriting – make sure it's neat and legible.

One to two days before the exam

- Recheck times, dates and venue.
- Actively review your notes and key facts.
- Exercise, eat sensibly and get a few good nights' sleep.

On the day

- Get a good night's sleep.
- Have a good meal, two to three hours before the start time.
- Arrive in good time.
- Spend a few minutes calming and focusing.

In the exam room

- Keep calm.
- Take a few minutes to read each question carefully. Don't jump to conclusions – think calmly about what each question means and the area it is focused on.
- Start with the question you feel most confident about. This helps your morale.
- By the same token, don't expend all your efforts on that one question – if you are expected to answer three questions then don't just answer two.
- Keep to time and spread your effort evenly on all opportunities to score marks.
- Once you have chosen a question, jot down any salient facts or key points. Then take five minutes to plan your answer – a spider diagram or a few notes may be enough to focus your ideas. Try to think in terms of 'why and how' not just 'facts'.
- You might find it useful to create a visual plan or map before writing your answer to help you remember to cover everything you need to address.

- Keep reminding yourself of the question and try not to wander off the point.
- Remember that quality of argument is more important than quantity of facts.
- Take 30–60-second breaks whenever you find your focus slipping (typically every 20 minutes).
- Make sure you reference properly – according to your university requirements.
- Watch your spelling and grammar – you could lose marks if you make too many errors.

→ *Final revision checklist*

❏ Have you revised the topics highlighted in the revision checklists?

❏ Have you attended revision classes and taken note of and/or followed up on your lecturers' advice about the exams or assessment process at your university?

❏ Can you answer the questions posed in this text satisfactorily? Don't forget to check sample answers on the website too.

❏ Have you read the additional material to make your answer stand out?

❏ Remember to criticise appropriately – based on evidence.

Test your knowledge by using the material presented in this text or on the website: **www.pearsoned.co.uk/psychologyexpress**

Glossary

360 degree appraisal: multi-rater, multi-source An appraisal made by all those involved with the individual (e.g. top management, immediate superior, peers, subordinates, self and customers).

anthropometric design Design concerned with the measurements of the proportions, size, and weight of the human body.

assessment centre A place at which a person is assessed to determine their suitability for particular roles.

bio-psycho-social approach General model or approach that posits that biological, psychological (which entails thoughts, emotions and behaviours) and social factors all play a significant role in human functioning.

bullying Negative behaviour being targeted at an individual, or individuals, repeatedly and persistently over time.

career counselling Counselling or mentoring/coaching on issues related to an individual's career.

coaching Teaching, training or development process through which an individual is supported while achieving a specific personal or professional result or goal.

cognitive ability The capacity to perform higher mental processes of reasoning, remembering, understanding and problem solving.

competency The ability to do something successfully or efficiently.

constructivist approach A psychological approach whereby problem solving is at the heart of learning, thinking and development. As people solve problems and discover the consequences of their actions through reflecting on past and immediate experiences, they construct their own understanding.

consultancy The act or business of providing professional or technical advice.

contingency approach A concept in management stating that there is no one universally applicable set of management principles by which to manage organisations.

counselling The provision of professional assistance and guidance in resolving personal or psychological problems.

employee relations Communications between management and employees concerning workplace decisions, grievances, conflicts, problem resolutions, unions, and issues of collective bargaining.

ergonomics Design factors, as for the workplace, intended to maximise productivity by minimising operator fatigue and discomfort.

ethics in counselling Ethical issues related to counselling including such issues as respect, confidentiality and privacy, permission to keep records, boundaries and use of appropriate assessment.

evaluation An act or instance of evaluating or appraising.

evidence-based practice (EBP) When a practitioner/clinician finds, appraises and uses the most current and valid research findings as the basis for clinical/business decisions.

halo effects and bias Type of cognitive bias where our perception of one personality trait influences how we view a person's entire personality.

human error The result of actions that fail to generate the intended outcomes. Human error can be categorised into slips, lapses and mistakes.

human error analysis Provides a systematic method of considering the possible errors and other human failures that may occur when performing a task.

human–machine interface (HMI) A communication device, typically a touchscreen or screen and keypad, between a computer system and a person.

human resource management (HRM) The policies and practices involved in carrying out the 'people' or human resources aspects of a management position, including recruiting, screening, training and appraising.

individual differences The variations from one person to another on any number of variables.

job analysis The process of studying and collecting information relating to operations and responsibilities of a specific job, and the characteristics needed for the job to be performed effectively.

motivation interventions Interventions designed to motivate individuals to change.

occupational health and safety A new paradigm in proactively preventing worker ill-health and promoting wellbeing at work.

organisational culture The values and behaviours that contribute to the unique social and psychological environment of an organisation.

organisational development and change A field of study that addresses change and how it affects organisations and the individuals within them.

organisational structure: mechanistic versus organic Mechanistic organisations have clear, well-defined, centralised, vertical hierarchies of command, authority and control, whereas within an organic structure organisations change their structures, roles and processes to respond and adapt to their environments.

participatory ergonomics Relies on actively involving workers in implementing ergonomic knowledge, procedures and changes with the intention of improving working conditions, safety, productivity, quality, morale and/or comfort.

performance-shaping factors Any factor that influences human performance. It may be external or internal to the person or factors in the work situation.

personal and professional development Those processes through which the organisation and individuals engage in ongoing learning to meet and address challenges and opportunities within agreed and identifiable boundaries.

personality The combination of characteristics or qualities that form an individual's distinctive character.

PEST PEST is a widely used tool that helps you analyse the Political, Economic, Sociocultural and Technological changes in your business environment.

psychological contract Represents the mutual beliefs, perceptions and informal obligations between an employer and an employee.

psychological resilience Individual's tendency to cope with stress and adversity.

psychometric tests Quantitative methods/tests used in order to measure an individual's competencies in specific areas of functioning.

psychometric tools Tools that include the measurement of knowledge, abilities, attitudes, personality traits and education.

rating scales (bars) An employee rating system that grades based on patterns or behaviours.

reductionist approach Refers to a theory that seems to over-simplify human behaviours or cognitive processes, and in doing so neglects to explain complexities that there may be.

researcher-practitioner divide Researchers and practitioners tend to come at problems from different backgrounds and cultures and hence may treat issues differently.

resistance to change The action taken by individuals or groups when they perceive an occurring change as a threat to them.

restriction of range Imposition of conditions by a researcher which limit the whole range of scores having been collected to a very constrained fraction of the total for observation.

return on investment (ROI) A performance measure used to evaluate the efficiency of an investment or to compare the efficiency of a number of different investments.

risk assessment A systematic process of evaluating the potential risks that may be involved in a specific activity or undertaking.

risk management The forecasting and evaluation of financial risks together with the identification of procedures to avoid or minimise their impact.

safety culture The ways in which safety is managed in the workplace.

selection and assessment process The process of assessing and selecting the appropriate candidate for a role.

stress State of mental or emotional strain or tension resulting from adverse or demanding circumstances.

systems approach A line of thought in the management field which stresses the interactive nature and interdependence of external and internal factors in an organisation.

theories of human knowledge acquisition Knowledge acquisition is the process of absorbing and storing new information. There are many theories of how this might be understood, including cognitive, behaviourist and experiential theories.

trade union An organised association of workers in a trade, group of trades, or profession, formed to protect and further their rights and interests.

tribunal A body established to settle certain types of dispute.

training design A training system that learners and trainers can implement to meet the learning goals.

training needs analysis (TNA) Assessment of the training requirements of a target group.

training objectives A statement that describes the desired outcome of a training activity.

training transfer The degree to which trainees effectively apply the knowledge, skills and attitudes gained in a training context to the job.

user-centred design Design philosophy where the end-user's needs, wants and limitations are a focus at all stages within the design process and development life cycle.

utility of the selection process The overall usefulness of a personnel selection or placement procedure. It is also concerned with costs.

workload The amount of work to be done by someone or something.

workplace conflict Specific type of conflict that occurs in workplaces.

References

Ackerman, P. L., & Beier, M. E. (2003). Intelligence, personality, and interests in the career choice process. *Journal of Career Assessment, 11*, 205–218.

Adams, J. S. (1963). Towards an understanding of inequality. *Journal of Abnormal and Normal Social Psychology, 67*, 422–436.

Ahlstrom, V., & Longo, K. (2003). *Human Factors Design Standard* (DOT/FAA/CT-03/05; HF-STD-001). Atlantic City International Airport, NJ: Federal Aviation Administration, WJH Technical Centre.

Anderson, J. R. (1983). *The architecture of cognition*. Cambridge, MA: Harvard University Press.

Anderson, N. (2007). The practitioner–researcher divide revisited: Strategic level bridges and the roles of IWO psychologists. *Journal of Occupational and Organisational Psychology, 80*, 175–183.

APA (2005). Evidence based practice in psychology. *American Psychologist, 61*(4), 271–285.

Apple Inc. (2012). *Apple Corporation Info*; available from http://investor.apple.com/faq .cfm?FaqSetID=6.

Arnold, J. (1996). The psychological contract: A concept in need of closer scrutiny? *European Journal of Work and Organizational Psychology, 5*(4), 511–520.

Arnold, J. (2004). The congruence problem in John Holland's theory of vocational decisions. *Journal of Occupational and Organizational Psychology, 77*(1), 95–113.

Arnold, J., & Randall, R. (Eds.) (2010). *Work psychology: Understanding human behaviour in the workplace* (5th ed.). Harlow: Pearson.

Arnold, J., Silvester, J., Patterson, F., Robertson, I., Cooper, C., & Burnes, B. (2005). *Work psychology: Understanding human behaviour in the workplace*. Harlow: Pearson Education.

Arthur, M. B., & Rousseau, D. M. (1996). *The boundaryless career: A new employment principle for a new organisational era*. Oxford: Oxford University Press.

Arthur, M. B., Hall, M. B., & Lawrence, B. S. (1989). *Handbook of Career Theory*. Cambridge: Cambridge University Press.

Arthur, W., Tubré, T., Paul, D. S., & Edens, P. S. (2003) Teaching effectiveness: The relationship between reactions and learning evaluation criteria. *Educational Psychology, 23*, 275–285.

Ashkanasy, N. M., Wilderom, C. P. M., & Peterson, M. F. (2000). *Handbook of organizational culture and climate*. London: Sage.

Baldwin, T. T., & Ford, J. K. (1988). Transfer of training: A review and directions for future research. *Personnel Psychology, 41*, 63–105.

Barley, S. R. (1989). Careers identities and institutions: The legacy of the Chicago school of sociology. In M. B. Arthur, D. T. Hall & B. S. Lawrence (Eds.), *Handbook of career theory* (pp. 41–65). Cambridge: Cambridge University Press.

Barrick, M. R., & Mount, M. K. (1991). The big five personality dimensions and job performance: A meta analysis. *Journal of Applied Psychology, 44*, 1–26.

Baruch, Y. (2004) *Managing careers: Theory and practice*. Harlow: Prentice Hall.

Beach, L. R., & Connolly, T. (2005). *The psychology of decision making: People in organizations. Foundations for organizational science* (2nd ed.). London: Sage.

Bicknell, A. (2002). Closing the e-learning loop. Abstract from paper presented at the UK Evaluation Society Conference, December, Cardiff.

Bicknell, A. (2006). Virtual alchemies: Can new learning technologies transform police training? Ph.D. thesis, University of Worcester/Coventry.

Bicknell, A., & Francis-Smythe, J. (2000). Virtual alchemies: Can learning technologies transform police training? *BPS Occupational Psychology Conference Proceedings*, 122–127.

161

References

Bicknell, A., & Vaughan, M. (2002). *Widening access to personal and professional development with e-learning in Police Services.* Queen's Research Award for Innovation in Police Training. London: Home Office.

Boerlijst, J. G., Munnichs, J. M. A., & Van der Heijden, B. I. J. M. (1998) The older worker in the organisation. In P. J. D. Drenth, H. Thierry & C. J. De Wolff (eds.), *Handbook of work and organisational psychology.* London: Psychology Press.

Bowman, J., & Wilson, J. P. (2008). Different roles, different perspectives: Perceptions about the purpose of training needs analysis. *Industrial and Commercial Training, 40*(1), 38–41.

Bradley, H., Erickson, M., Stephenson, C., & Williams, S. (2000). *Myths at work.* Oxford: Blackwell.

Briggs-Myers, I., & Briggs, K. C. (1985). *Myers–Briggs Type Indicator (MBTI).* Palo Alto, CA: Consulting Psychologists Press.

British Psychological Society (BPS) (2012). *The British Psychological Society*; available from http://www.bps.org.uk/

Brousseau, K. R., Driver, M. J., Eneroth, K., & Larsson, R. (1996). Career pandemonium: Realigning organizations and individuals. *Academy of Management Executive, 10*(4), 52–66.

Budd, J. W., & Mumford, K. (2004). Trade unions and family-friendly policies in Britain. *Industrial and Labor Relations Review, 57*(2), 204–222.

Burke, M. J., Borucki, C. C., & Kaufman, J. D. (2002). Contemporary perspectives on the study of psychological climate: A commentary. *European Journal of Work and Organizational Psychology, 11*(3), 325–340.

Burwell, R., & Chen, C. P. (2006). Applying the principles and techniques of solution-focused therapy to career counselling. *Counselling Psychology Quarterly, 19*(2), 189–203.

Cameron, E., & Green, M. (2012). *Making sense of change management.* London: Kogan Page.

Carless, S. A., & Wintle, J. (2007). Applicant attraction: The role of recruiter function, work life balance policies and career salience. *International Journal of Selection and Assessment, 15*(4), 394–404.

Carroll, M. (1996). *Counselling supervision: Theory, skills and practice.* London: Cassell.

Cattell, R. B., & Cattell, H. E. P. (1995). Personality structure and the new fifth edition of the 16PF. *Educational and Psychological Measurement, 55*(6), 926–937.

Chapman, A. (2010). *Equity theory*; available from http://www.businessballs.com/adamsequitytheory.htm.

Chapman, A. (2012). *Organizational change, training, and learning*; available from http://www.businessballs.com/organizationalchange.htm

CIPD (2012). *Organisational development*; available from http://www.cipd.co.uk/hr-resources/factsheets/organisation-development.aspx

CIPD Staff (2013). *Performance appraisal factsheet.* Available at http://www.cipd.co.uk/hr-resources/factsheets/performance-appraisal.aspx; last accessed 20 April 2013.

Collin, A., & Watts, A. G. (1996). The death and transfiguration of career – and of career guidance? *British Journal of Guidance and Counselling, 24*(3), 385–398.

Costa, P. T., McCrae, R. R., & Dye, D. A. (1991). Facet scales for Agreeableness and Conscientiousness: A revision of the NEO Personality Inventory. *Personality and Individual Differences, 12*, 887–898.

Cox, E., Bachkirova, T., & Clutterbuck, D. (2010). *The complete handbook of coaching.* London: Sage.

Crowley-Henry, M., & Weir, D. (2007). The international protean career: Four women's narratives. *Journal of Organizational Change Management, 20*(2), 245–258.

Daft, R., Murphy, J., & Willmott, H. (2010). *Organization theory and design.* Andover: Cengage Learning EMEA.

Dann, S. (1995). Gender differences in self-perceived success. *Women in Management Review, 10*(8), 11–18.

De Vos, A., & Freese, C. (2011). Sensemaking during organizational entry: Changes in newcomer information seeking and the relationship with psychological contract fulfilment. *Journal of Occupational and Organizational Psychology, 84*, 288–314.

Demaiter, E. I., & Adams, T. L. (2009). "I really didn't have any problems with the male-female thing until...": Successful women's experiences in IT organizations. *Canadian Journal of Sociology, 34*(1): 31–53.

Denby, S. (2010). The importance of training needs analysis. *Industrial and Commercial Training, 42*(3), 147–150.

DirectGov (2012). *Bullying in the workplace*; available from http://www.direct.gov.uk/en/Employment/ResolvingWorkplaceDisputes/DiscriminationAtWork/DG_10026670

Donaldson-Feilder, E., Yarker, J., & Lewis, R. (2011). *Preventing stress in organisations: How to develop positive managers.* Chichester: Wiley-Blackwell.

Endsley, M. R. (2000). Theoretical underpinnings of situation awareness: A critical review. In M. R. Endsley & D. J. Garland (Eds.), *Situation awareness analysis and measurement* (pp. 3–28). Mahwah, NJ: Lawrence Erlbaum Associates.

Evans, S. (2012). Analysis of the relationship that exists between organizational culture, motivation and performance. *Problems of Management in the 21st Century, 3*, 106–119.

Facebook (2012). Facebook mission statement; available from https://www.facebook.com/facebook/info

Fitts, P. M. (1964). Perceptual motor skill learning. In A. W. Melton (Ed.), *Categories of human learning* (pp. 243–285). New York: Academic Press.

Flanagan, J. C. (1954). The critical incident technique. *Psychological Bulletin, 51*(4), 327–358.

Fletcher, C. (2001). Performance appraisal and management: The developing research agenda. *Journal of Occupational and Organizational Psychology, 74*, 473–487.

Fletcher, C. (2004). Appraisal and feedback: Making performance review work (3rd ed.). London: Institute of Personnel and Development.

Fletcher, C. (2008). *Appraisal, feedback and development: Making performance review work* (4th ed.). London: Routledge.

Fouad, N. A. (2007). Work and vocational psychology: Theory, research and applications. *Annual Review of Psychology, 58*, 543–564.

Francis-Smythe, J., Haase, S., Thomas, E., et al. (2013). Development and validation of the Career Competencies Indicator (CCI). *Journal of Career Assessment, 21*(2), 227–248.

Freese, C., & Schalk, R. (1996). Implications of differences in psychological contracts for human resource management. *European Journal of Work and Organizational Psychology, 5*(4), 501–509.

French, J. R. P., Caplan, R. D., & Harrison, R. V. (1982). *The mechanisms of job stress and strain.* Chichester: John Wiley & Sons.

Furnham, A. (2005). *The psychology of behaviour at work: The individual in the organization.* Hove: Psychology Press.

Gagné, R. M., Briggs, L. J., & Wager, W. W. (1992). *Principles of instructional design* (4th ed.). Fort Worth, TX: Harcourt Brace Jovanovich.

Gallos, J. (1989). Exploring women's development: Implications for theory, practice and research. In M. B. Arthur, D. T. Hall & B. S. Lawrence (Eds.), *Handbook of career theory* (pp. 110–132). Cambridge: Cambridge University Press.

Ghiselli, E. E. (1966). *The validity of occupational aptitude tests.* New York: Wiley.

Goldstein, I. L., & Ford, J. K. (2002). *Training in organisations* (4th ed.). Belmont, CA: Wadsworth.

Gottfredson, L. S. (1981). Circumscription and compromise: A developmental theory of occupational aspirations. *Journal of Counselling Psychology Monograph, 28*, 545–579.

Guba, E. G., & Lincoln, Y. S. (1989). *Fourth generation evaluation.* London: Sage.

Hackman, J. R., & Oldham, G. R. (1980). *Work re-design.* Reading, MA: Addison-Wesley.

Hakim, C. (2006). Women, careers and work life preferences. *British Journal of Guidance and Counselling, 34*(3), 279–293.

Hall, D. T. (1976). *Careers in Organisations.* Glenview, IL: Scott Foresman.

References

Hall, D. T. (1996). Protean careers of the 21st century. *Academy of Management Executive*, *10*(4), 8–16.

Hall, D. T. (2002). *Careers in and out of organizations*. Thousand Oaks, CA: Sage.

Hall, D. T., & Mirvis, P. H. (1995). The new career contract: Developing the whole person at midlife and beyond. *Journal of Vocational Behavior, 47*, 269–289.

Harris, D. (2011). *Human performance on the flight deck*. Aldershot: Ashgate.

Harris, D., & Harris, F. J. (2004). Predicting the successful transfer of technology between application areas: A critical evaluation of the human component in the system. *Technology in Society, 26*, 551–565.

Health and Safety Executive (2002). *Upper limb disorders in the workplace* (HSG60). London: HMSO.

Health and Safety Executive (2011). *Five steps to risk assessment*; available from www.hse.gov.uk/pubns/indg163.pdf.

Hendrick, K., & Benner, L. (1987). *Investigating accidents with S-T-E-P*. New York: Marcel-Decker.

Herold, D. M., Fedor, D. B., & Caldwell, S. D. (2007). Beyond change management: A multilevel investigation of contextual and personal influences on employees' commitment to change. *Journal of Applied Psychology, 92*, 942–951.

Herriot, P. (2001). *The employment relationship: A psychology perspective*. Hove: Routledge.

Herzberg, F., Mausner, B., & Snyderman, B. (1959). *The motivation to work*. New York: John Wiley & Sons.

Holland, J. (1996) Exploring careers with a typology: What we have learned and some new directions. *American Psychologist, 51*(4), 397–406.

Hollnagel, E. (1993). *Human reliability analysis: Context and control*. London: Academic Press.

Honey, P., & Mumford, A. (1992). *The manual of learning styles* (revised ed.). Maidenhead: Peter Honey.

Hopson, B., & Adams, J. (1976). *Transition: Understanding and managing personal change*. Retrieved 31 January 2013 from http://www.eoslifework.co.uk/transprac.htm.

Howard, G. (2000). Legal aspects of fitness for work. In K. Palmer (Ed.), *Fitness for work: The medical aspects* (pp. 26–41). Oxford: Oxford University Press.

Huang, Q., & Sverke, M. (2007). Women's occupational career patterns over 27 years: Relations to family of origin, life careers, and wellness. *Journal of Vocational Behavior, 70*(2), 369–397.

Hui-Min, K. (2009). Understanding relationships between academic staff and administrators: An organizational culture perspective. *Journal of Higher Education Policy and Management, 31*(1), 43–54.

Hull, K. E., & Nelson, R. L. (2000). Assimilation, choice or constraint? Testing theories of gender differences in the careers of lawyers. *Social Forces, 79*(1), 229–264.

Hunter, J. E., & Hunter, R. F. (1984). Validity and utility of alternate predictors of job performance. *Psychological Bulletin, 96*, 72–98.

Hutchins, E. (1995). How a cockpit remembers its speeds. *Cognitive Science, 19*, 265–288.

Institute of Directors and Health and Safety Executive (2011). *Leading health and safety at work*; available from http://www.hse/.gov.uk/pubns/indg417.pdf.

Jafri, H. (2011). Influence of psychological contract breach on organizational commitment. *Synergy, 9*(2), 19–30.

Jaramillo, F., Mulki, J. P., & Boles, J. S. (2011). Workplace stressors, job attitude and job behaviours: Is interpersonal conflict the missing link? *Journal of Personal Selling and Sales Management, 31*(3), 339–356.

Jewell, L. N. (1998). *Contemporary industrial and organisational psychology*. Pacific Grove, CA: Brookes/Cole.

Johns, G. (1992). *Organizational behavior*. New York: HarperCollins.

Johnson, A. (2011). Not an easy task: Dramatic improvement starts with safety culture. *Safety Culture*, 48–51.

Johnson, G., Scholes, K., & Whittington, R. (2008). *Exploring corporate strategy* (8th ed.). London: Pearson Education.

Jome, L. M., & Tokar, D. M. (1998). Dimensions of masculinity and major choice traditionality. *Journal of Vocational Behavior, 52*, 120–134.

Jones, C., and DeFillippi, R. J. (1996). Back to the future in film: Combining industry and self-knowledge to meet career challenges of the 21st century. *Academy of Management Executive, 10*(4), 91.

Kahneman, D. (2011). *Thinking fast and slow*. London: Allen Lane.

Karasek, R. A. (1979). Job demands, job decision latitude and mental strain: Implications for job re-design. *Administrative Science Quarterly, 24*, 285–308.

Klein, G. (2008). Naturalistic decision-making. *Human Factors, 50*(3), 456–460.

Kluger, A. N., & DeNisi, A. (1998). Feedback interventions: Toward the understanding of a double-edged sword. *Current Directions in Psychological Science, 7*(3), 67–72.

Kolb, D. A. (1984). *Experiential learning*. Englewood Cliffs, NJ: Prentice Hall.

Latham, G. P., & Pinder, C. C. (2005). Work motivation theory and research at the dawn of the twenty-first century. *Annual Review of Psychology, 56*, 485–516.

Latham, G. P., Sulsky, L. M., & MacDonald, H. A. (2008). Performance management. In P. Boxall, S. Purcell, & P. Wright (Eds.), *Oxford Handbook of Human Resource Management*. Oxford: Oxford University Press.

Levinson, D. J. (1978). *The seasons of a man's life*. New York: Knopf.

Levinson, D. J., & Levinson, J. D. (1996). *The seasons of a woman's life*. New York: Ballantine.

Lewin, K. (1951). *Field theory in social science*. London: Harper Row.

Liebig, B., & Sansonetti, S. (2004). Career paths. *Current Sociology, 52*(3), 371–406.

Locke, E. A., & Latham, G. P. (1984). *Goal setting: A motivational technique that works*. London: Prentice Hall.

Lord, R. G., Hanges, P. J., & Godfrey, E. G. (2003). Integrating neural networks into decision-making and motivational theory: Rethinking VIE theory. *Canadian Psychology, 44*(1), 21–38.

Machin, M. A., Fogharty, G. J., & Bannon, S. F. (2009). Predicting employees' commitment and support for organisational change. *Australian and New Zealand Journal of Organisational Psychology, 2*, 10–18.

Mafi, S. L. (2000). Managing the HRD function and service quality: A call for a new approach. *Human Resources Development Quarterly, 11*(1), 81–86.

Mager, R. F. (1962). *Preparing instructional objectives*. Palo Alto, CA: Fearon.

Maguire, M. (2001). Methods to support human-centred design. *International Journal of Human-Computer Studies, 55*, 587–634.

Makin, P., Cooper, C., & Cox, C. (1996). *Organisations and the Psychological Contract*. Leicester: British Psychological Society.

Marks, M. L. (2006). Workplace recovery after mergers, acquisitions, and downsizing: Facilitating individual adaptation to major organizational transformations. *Organizational Dynamics, 35*, 384–398.

Maslow, A. H. (1954). *Motivation and personality*. New York: Harper & Row.

Mathews, J. (2009). Models of change management: A reanalysis. *Journal of Business* Strategy, 4(2), 7–17.

Maurer, T. J., Mitchell, D. R. D., & Barbeite, E. G. (2002). Predictors of attitudes towards 360-degree feedback system and involvement in post-feedback management and development activity. *Journal of Occupational and Organizational Psychology, 75*(1), 87–107.

McCormick, E. J., Jeanneret, P. R., & Mechan, R. C. (1972). A study of job characteristics and job dimensions as based on the position analysis questionnaire (PAQ). *Journal of Applied Psychology, 56*, 347–368.

McDonald, P., Brown, K., & Bradley, L. (2005). Have traditional career paths given way to protean ones?: Evidence from senior managers in the Australian public sector. *Career Development International, 10*(2), 109–129.

McGhee, W., & Thayer, P. (1961). *Training in business industry*. New York: John Wiley & Sons.

Metropolitan Police (2012). *About the Met*; available from http://content.met.police.uk/Site/About.

References

Meyer, J. P., & Herscovitch, L. (2001). Commitment in the workplace: Toward a general model. *Human Resource Management Review, 11*, 299–326.

Miller, G. A. (1956). The magical number seven, plus or minus two: Some limits on our capacity for processing information. *Psychological Review, 63*(2), 81–97.

Millward, L. (2005). *Understanding occupational and organizational psychology.* London: Sage.

Milner, P., & Palmer, S. (1998). *Integrative stress counselling: A humanistic problem-focused approach.* London: Sage.

Mullins, L. J. (2007). *Management and organisational behaviour.* London: Prentice Hall.

Nadin, S. J., & Williams, C. C. (2012). Psychological contract violation beyond an employees' perspective: The perspective of employers. *Employee Relations, 34*(2), 110–125.

Napier, N. K., & Latham, G. P. (1986). Outcome expectancies of people who conduct performance appraisals. *Personnel Psychology, 39*, 827–837.

National Career Development Association (NCDA) (2007). *Code of ethics.* Retrieved 31 January 2013 from http://www.ncda.org/aws/NCDA/asset_manager/get_file/3395.

Neault, R. A., & Pickerell, D. A. (2011). Career engagement: Bridging career counselling and employee engagement. *Journal of Employment Counselling, 48*, 185–188.

NSPCC (2012). *About the NSPCC*; available from http://www.nspcc.org.uk/what-we-do/about-the-nspcc/about-the-NSPCC_wdh71771.html.

Oborne, D. J. (1992). *Ergonomics at work.* Chichester: John Wiley.

O'Dea, A., & Flin, R. (2001). Site managers and safety leadership in the offshore oil and gas industry. *Safety Science, 37*(1), 39–57.

O*NET Resource Centre (2003). Retrieved 31 January 2013 from http://www.onetcenter.org.

Palmer, R. (2006). The identification of learning needs in Wilson, J. (Ed.), *Human resource development: Learning and training for individuals and organisations* (pp. 137–155). London: Kogan Page.

Parmelli, E., Flodgren, G., Beyer, F., et al. (2011). The effectiveness of strategies to change organisational culture to improve healthcare performance: A systematic review. *Implementation Science, 6*(33), 1–8.

Personnel Today. (2006). *Management style: too cruel to be kind.* Retrieved from http://www.personneltoday.com/hr/management-styles-too-cruel-to-be-kind/

Pinder, C. C. (2008). *Work motivation in organizational psychology* (2nd ed.). Hove: Psychology Press.

Prediger, D. J. (1982). Dimensions underlying Holland's hexagon: Missing link between interests and occupations? *Journal of Vocational Behaviour, 21*, 259–287.

Pressman, R. S. (1992). Cited in J. Arnold & R. Randall (Eds.), *Work psychology: Understanding human behaviour in the workplace.* Harlow: Pearson Education, 2010.

PwC (2012). *PwC mission*; available from http://www.pwc.com/us/en/retail-consumer/practice-overview-mission-statement.jhtml.

Pyman, A., Holland, P., Teicher, J., et al. (2010). Industrial relations climate, employee voice and managerial attitudes to unions: An Australian study. *British Journal of Industrial Relations, 48*(2), 460–480.

Quick, J., Quick, J., Nelson, D., & Hurrell, J. (1997). *Preventative stress management in organisations.* Washington, DC: APA.

Quinn-Patton, M. (1997). *Utilization-focused evaluation* (3rd ed.). London: Sage.

Quiñones, M. A., & Ehrenstein, A. (1997). *Training for a rapidly changing workplace: Applications of psychological research.* Washington, DC: American Psychological Association.

Rahmati, V., Darouian, S., & Ahmadinia, H. (2012). A review on the effect of culture, structure, technology and behavior on organizations. *Australian Journal of Basic and Applied Sciences, 6*(3), 128–135.

Randhawa, G. (2007). *Human resource management.* New Delhi: Atlantic Publishers and Distributors.

Reason, J. (1990). *Human error.* Cambridge: Cambridge University Press.

Reeves, W. (1999). *Learner-centred design.* London: Sage.

Robbins, S. P., & Barnwell, N. (2006). *Organisation theory: Concepts and cases*. Australia: Pearson Education.

Rouse, W., & Morris, N. (1987). Conceptual design of a human error tolerant interface for complex engineering systems. *Automatica, 23*(2), 231–235.

Rousseau, D. M. (2004). Psychological contracts in the workplace: Understanding the ties that motivate. *Academy of Management Executive, 18*(1), 120–127.

Saari, L. M., Johnson, T. R., McLaughlin, S. D., & Zimmerle, D. M. (1988). A survey of management education practices in US companies. *Personnel Psychology, 41*, 731–743.

Saffo, P. (2000). The consumer spectrum. In T. Winnograd (Ed.), *Bringing design to software* (pp. 87–99). London: Addison Wesley.

Sargent, L. D., & Domberger, S. R. (2007). Exploring the development of a Protean career orientation: Values and image violations. *Career Development International, 12*(6), 545–564.

Saunders, M. N. K., Thornhill, A., & Lewis, P. (2010). *Research methods for business students* (5th ed.). Mahwah, NJ: Prentice Hall.

Savickas, M. L. (2002). Career construction: A developmental theory of vocational behaviour. In D. Brown and Associates (Eds.), *Career choice and development* (4th ed., pp. 149–205). San Francisco, CA: Jossey-Bass.

Savickas, M. L. (2005). The theory and practice of career construction. In S. D. Brown & R. W. Lent (Eds.), *Career development and counselling: Putting theory and research to work* (pp. 42–69). Hoboken, NJ: John Wiley & Sons.

Schein, E. H. (1978). *Career dynamics: Matching individual and organisational needs*. Reading, MA: Addison-Wesley.

Schein, E. H. (1982). Individuals and careers. In J. W. Lorsch (Ed.), *Handbook of Organizational Behaviour* (pp. 155–171). Upper Saddle River, NJ: Prentice Hall.

Schein, E. H. (1993). *Career anchors: Discovering your real values*. San Diego, CA: Pfeiffer & Company.

Schmidt, F. L., & Hunter, J. E. (1998). The validity and utility of selection methods in personnel psychology: Practical and theoretical implications of 85 years of research. *Psychological Bulletin, 124*(2), 262–274.

Schmidt, F. L., Gast-Rosenberg, I. F., & Hunter, J. E. (1980). Validity generalisation results for computer programmers. *Journal of Applied Psychology, 65*, 463–661.

Seale, C. (1999). *The quality of qualitative research*. London: Sage.

Searle, R. H. (2003). *Selection and assessment: A critical text*. Basingstoke: Palgrave Macmillan.

Sellitto, C. (2011). Organisational structure: Some observations on the importance of informal advice and trust networks. *International Journal of Interdisciplinary Sciences, 6*(2), 23–34.

Senge, P. (1993). *The fifth discipline: The art and practice of the learning organization*. London: Century Business.

Senior, B., & Fleming, J. (2006). *Organisational change*. Harlow: Pearson Education.

Senior, B., & Swailes, S. (2010). *Organizational change* (4th ed.). Harlow: Prentice Hall.

Shakel, B. (1991). Usability – context, framework, design and evaluation. In B. Shakel & S. Richardson (Eds.), *Human factors for informatics usability* (pp. 21–38). Cambridge: Cambridge University Press.

Shimmin, S., & Wallis, D. (1994). Fifty years of occupational psychology in Britain. Leicester: British Psychological Society.

Shin, J., Taylor, M. S., & Seo, M-G. (2012). Resources for change: The relationships of organisational inducements and psychological resilience to employees' attitudes and behaviours toward organisational change. *Academy of Management Journal, 55*(3), 727–748.

Smith, P. C., & Kendall, L. M. (1963). Retranslation of expectations: An approach to the construction of unambiguous anchors for rating scales. *Journal of Applied Psychology, 4*, 149–155.

Smith, W. J., Harrington, K. V., & Houghton, J. D. (2000). Predictors of performance appraisal discomfort. *Public Personnel Management, 29*(1), 1–22.

Sonnentag, S. (2000). Working in a network context – What are we talking about? Comment on Symon. *Journal of Occupational and Organizational Psychology, 73*, 415–418.

References

Stacey, R. D. (2001). *Complex responsive processes in organizations: Learning and knowledge creation*. London: Routledge.

Standish Group (1995). *The Standish Group Report*. Boston, MA: Standish Group.

Stanton, N. A. (2003). Editorial: On the cost-effectiveness of ergonomics. *Applied Ergonomics, 34*, 407–411.

Stanton, N., & Young, M. (1999). *A guide to methodology in ergonomics: Designing for human use*. London: Taylor & Francis.

Steers, R. M., Mowday, R. T., & Shapiro, D. L. (2004).The future of work motivation theory. *Academy of Management Review, 29*, 379–387.

Sullivan, S. E. (1999). The changing nature of careers: A review and research agenda. *Journal of Management, 25*(3), 457–484.

Super, D. (1957). *Psychology of careers*. New York: Harper & Brothers.

Sutherland, V. (2000). *The management of safety*. London: Sage.

Swailes, S. (2004). Commitment to change: Profiles of commitment and in-role performance. *Personnel Review, 33*, 187–204.

Symon, G. (2000). Information and communication technologies and the network organisation: A critical analysis. *Journal of Occupational and Organizational Psychology, 73*, 389–414.

Taber, B. J., Hartung, P. J., Briddick, H., et al. (2011). Career style interview: A contextualised approach to career counselling. *Career Development Quarterly, 59*, 274–287.

Thaler, R., & Sunstein, C. (2008). *Nudge*. London: Yale University Press.

Tharanou, P. (2001). The relationship of training motivation to participation in training and development. *Journal of Occupational and Organizational Psychology, 74*(5), 599–622.

Tremblay, M. A., Blanchard, C. M., Taylor, S., et al. (2009). Work extrinsic and intrinsic motivation scale: Its value for organizational psychology research. *Canadian Journal of Behavioural Science, 41*(4), 213–226.

Tsung-Chih, W., Chi-Hsiang, C., & Chin-Chung, L. (2008). A correlation among safety leadership, safety climate and safety performance. *Journal of Loss Prevention in the Process Industries, 21*(3), 307–318.

Turner, N., & Williams, L. (2005). *The ageing workforce*. London: Corporate Partners Research Programme – The Work Foundation.

US Department of Labor (1991). *Dictionary of occupational titles* (4th ed.). Washington, DC: US Government Printing Office.

Vroom, V. H. (1964). *Work and motivation*. San Francisco, CA: Jossey-Bass.

Weick, K. E., & Quinn, R. E. (1999). Organizational change and development. *Annual Review of Psychology, 50*, 361–388.

Weiner, E., & Curry, R. (1980). Flight deck automation: Promises and problems. *Ergonomics, 23*, 995–1011.

Whittingham, R. B. (2004). To err is human. In R. Whittingham (Ed.), *The blame machine* (pp. 3–11). Oxford: Elsevier Butterworth-Heinemann.

Wickens, C. (1992). *Engineering psychology and human performance* (2nd ed.). New York: HarperCollins.

Wickens, C., Hollands, J., Parasuraman, R., & Banbury, S. (2012). *Engineering Psychology and Human Performance* (4th ed.). Harlow: Pearson.

Wilensky, H. L. (1961). Careers, lifestyles, and social integration. *International Social Science Journal, 12*(4), 553–558.

Woods, S. A., & West, M. A. (2010). *The psychology of work and organizations*. Andover: Cengage Learning EMEA.

York, J., & Pendharkar, P. (2004). Human–computer interaction issues for mobile computing in a variable work context. *International Journal of Human–Computer Studies, 60*, 771–797.

Index

Note: Page numbers in **bold** refer to terms defined in the glossary.